LIGHTS UP!

A Collection of One-Act Plays for Kids

by
Margo Haas

D1738036

Plays by Margo Haas

The Missing Choir of Soda Springs

Chilly Dog and Other Plays (collection)

Lost in the Bermuda Triangle

Christmas at the Wiley Diner

Texaco Star

Sacred Hearts

The Christmas Cowboy

Neighbors

Books

In This Sleep of Death

Among the Common

To Thea and Casper with love

Table of Contents

INTRODUCTION

Why Lights Up!

After years of teaching playwriting and directing children's theatre, I came to realize too few plays out there have all-kid casts with average, contemporary child characters. There are plenty of traditional fables, fairy tales, fractured fairy tales, modern fairy tales, fantasies and anthropomorphic characters available (which certainly have their merits and I have, in fact, included one in this book), but what I found is that kids really *love* playing *kids*. Because children are so wildly talented by nature when it comes to acting, they pull off adult roles with impressive panache. But really, truly, they shine their brightest when it comes to playing a child.

Lights Up! is a fun-filled collection of seven short plays about everyday kids in various predicaments and what they do to resolve them. All parts are written for children, with the exception of *The Great Potato Trial* (which features an all-vegetable cast,) and *Dottie's Paradise* which has one rabbit character. All the plays are written with age flexibility in mind, production needs fluid and gender-neutral casting in most cases. Traditional girl and boy names can be changed to fit your casting and production needs. In two separate Cleveland productions of *The Hearts of Philly*, they were performed with all-female casts, but it is not necessary.

This book is for directors and teachers—both classroom and home school educators, drama clubs, Scout troops, afterschool facilitators, for parents and caregivers and for children's theatre. It's intended to be fun and engaging, and is geared for ages eight years old and up. Plays can contain a mix of ages, and several of the plays allow for extras.

Small budget? No performance space? This anthology of royalty-free plays has been made affordable enough to order multiple copies for your actors, more economical than paying royalties for each performance. And if you don't have access to a stage, no worries. I have staged plays in a garage, on a grassy knoll, a porch, in a classroom, a hallway and a gym. An acquaintance of mine recently staged a full-length play in his kitchen (the play was set in a kitchen) with the audience seated in the adjacent dining room. Props and set can be as simple or as elaborate as your production budget (or no budget) allows.

I have included set, prop, sound and costume lists following each play, with some suggestions on making your own set and prop pieces if real ones are not available.

Okay, time to get started! Lights up!

SYNOPSES

THE TALENT SHOW (5 char, extras optional)
Camp Big Horn is holding its annual talent show and the campers from Grey Wolf Cabins are determined to win, breaking the cabin's fifty-year losing streak. They look on track to win when everything suddenly changes and they now have only hours to find new talent.

THE RADIO GHOST (5 char, extras optional)
A 100-year old radio provides more than music, and the kids playing it get more than they bargained for in this tingling time-travel mystery.

THE GREAT POTATO TRIAL (9 char, extras optional)
Sparks fly in Veggie Run, a farming community, when the entire potato crop has been destroyed, and the accused is ringleader Sweet Potato herself. An all-vegetable cast.

HAPPY BIRTHDAY, BONNIE MACDOUGALL (4 char)

It appears to be her birthday, all right, considering all the gifts in the attic for her, but just who is Bonnie MacDougall? It takes some real sleuths to unravel the mystery.

DOTTIE IN PARADISE (4 char)

A beautiful pet rabbit is in desperate need of love and proper care, but providing that has become a difficult challenge for one family.

THE HEARTS OF PHILLY (6 char, extras optional)

A group of friends are about to lose their secret meeting place. Friendships are set on edge when a new person shows up who tests what real friendships are about.

A PENNY FOR YOUR THOUGHTS (3 char)

It takes practice and know-how to flip a penny mid-air and catch it, and Robin makes sure everyone in the park knows it. But the bragging takes a turn when competition arrives.

THE TALENT SHOW

CAST OF CHARACTERS

(Age range is 8-14 years old)

OSCAR

FAWN

TREAT

BEANIE

PATTI

EXTRAS - optional

PLACE

Camp Big Horn, somewhere in the U.S.A.

TIME

The present, summer.

SETTING

A cabin.

THE TALENT SHOW

A cabin at Camp Bighorn.

The room has a table and some chairs. A door Stage Right leads to the outside. A poster hangs on the wall announcing the annual talent show.

AT RISE: OSCAR is doing vocal warmups. BEANIE is off to the side banging on a plastic pail. PATTI and FAWN are working on posters.

OSCAR: Mah-a-eee-mah-a-eeeeeeeee.

PATTI: You sound like a dying goat, Oscar.

OSCAR: Warm-ups! I've gotta keep my throat in shape for the big night.

PATTI: And Beanie's hitting a big plastic pail. Why?

BEANIE: Um, because we needed at least two people to enter the talent show and we're the only ones who volunteered.

PATTI: But with a plastic pail?

BEANIE: Percussion! Drum! I had to do something and I'm sure not gonna sing.

OSCAR: Admit it, you guys, together we sound great.

BEANIE: Just one more day till the Beanie and Oscar duo—

OSCAR: Oscar and Beanie.

BEANIE: Beanie and Oscar.

OSCAR: Oscar and Beanie.

BEANIE: Beanie and Oscar.

OSCAR: Oscar and Beanie.

PATTI: Well, which is it?! We're making more posters. We need to know.

BEANIE: Ok, Oscar and Beanie then.

PATTI: I hope the Grey Wolf cabins win the talent show. How awesome would that be? I mean, the Grey Wolf cabins have never won the Big Horn talent show, ever. And it's been here since 1962.

BEANIE: It's like our cabins are jinxed or something. How does that happen? It's different kids every year.

OSCAR: Just bad luck. But that's all gonna change tomorrow night.

BEANIE: Yes, it is.

OSCAR: Beanie and I are gonna break that losing streak and take home the Big Horn Camp talent trophy for Grey Wolf cabins.

ALL: Yay!!!!

PATTI: You don't actually get to take the trophy home, though. But it doesn't matter, just so we win!

BEANIE: How could we not win with Oscar singing? He should be on TV.

OSCAR: (*Puffed up, formal*) Thank you, Beanie. I'm so very humbled by your comment.

PATTI: (*To Oscar*) Oh, you are not. You have a good voice—well, a great voice—but you are always telling us that.

OSCAR: Well, true. But I do, so it's not bragging. We'll win, just wait, a perfect ending to two weeks of fun in the wilderness.

(Enter TREAT)

TREAT: Hey, guys.

PATTI: Hi, Treat.

OSCAR: Treat, we're just gonna start practicing.

TREAT: Well, you have to do it someplace else. Ms. Meadows just told me the other group needs this cabin now.

BEANIE: But we just got here.

TREAT: You had an hour.

OSCAR: There's no place else to practice without everybody hearing us.

PATTI: Maybe you shouldn't have spent the whole hour warming-up.

OSCAR: Warming up is important!

TREAT: We're just glad you two volunteered for the talent show, since we were forced to have somebody from Grey Wolf cabins sign up.

OSCAR: Glad to help, my minions.

FAWN: (*To Patti*) I'm going to go hang these posters up in the dining hall.

PATTI: Okay, Fawn, thanks.

(FAWN exits with posters.)

BEANIE: You should have entered the talent contest too, Patti.

PATTI: Me? I can balance a glass of water on my head. Not very entertaining.

TREAT: You're right about that.

OSCAR: Fawn then. Ha, ha.

BEANIE: Fawn! She would pass out up on stage.

OSCAR: Right? She's afraid of everything.

BEANIE: She never talks.

TREAT: I know. Why was she here just now?

PATTI: She was doing posters with me.

OSCAR: She never wants to do anything the rest of us are doing.

PATTI: Yes, she does.

TREAT: She wouldn't do archery yesterday. Mr. Dawson kept trying to talk her into it.

OSCAR: Or fishing.

PATTI: She's just shy. It's not a crime.

TREAT: I think today was the first time I heard her talk.

PATTI: So, why didn't *you* volunteer for the show, Treat?

TREAT: Someone had to be the stage manager.

PATTI: Yeah, whatever.

OSCAR: Well, tonight Beanie and I are sleeping under the stars with the Black Bear cabins. Did anybody else sign up to sleep outside?

TREAT: No.

PATTI: It gets too cold at night.

TREAT: Ok, we've got this place one more time. Tomorrow morning. Eight o'clock sharp. It's your last chance to practice before the show.

OSCAR: Got it.

TREAT: Everybody be here.

PATTI: Okay.

OSCAR: Meee-meeee-meee. Eight o'clock!

(*THEY all start to exit.*)

PATTI: (*Teasing*) Don't get eaten by coyotes.

BEANIE: Ha, ha. Funny.

PATTI: It won't be when they come out.

LIGHTS UP!

OSCAR: There's no coyotes around here. Mr. Dawson would've said so.

PATTI: Don't you hear them at night?

BEANIE: No. What do they sound like?

PATTI: Like coyotes.

TREAT: Just ignore her. It's probably just mountain lions.

OSCAR: We're not even near any mountains.

(On exit)

TREAT: Black bears then.

BEANIE: There's none of them either.

PATTI: You hope.

Blackout
End of Scene One

Scene Two

The next morning. FAWN and
PATTI are alone.

PATTI: *(Rambling)* Fawn, do you realize we will
be part of Camp Big Horn history when Oscar
and Beanie win the trophy tonight? They, well,
we, will be the ones who break the spell. I mean,
I know you and I aren't actually performing, but
we *are* the Grey Wolves and helped select the
talent and are working on the show. The prize
will be all of ours really. Oh, this is so exciting!

FAWN: Yeah.

PATTI: Maybe it'll be on TV.

FAWN: *(Doubtful)* Hmmm.

PATTI: Aren't you excited, Fawn?

FAWN: Yeah.

PATTI: Where is everybody? Treat is always early, where is he?

FAWN: They'll be here.

PATTI: Maybe they overslept. But how could anybody oversleep with the bugle blowing at seven o'clock?

(TREAT rushes in out of breath.)

TREAT: Have you seen them?

PATTI: Oscar and Beanie?

TREAT: Of course, Oscar and Beanie! Who else?

PATTI: Where are they?

TREAT: That's what I just asked you!

PATTI: I don't know.

TREAT: You don't know what?

PATTI: Where they are! You're the stage manager.

TREAT: Fawn, have you seen them?

FAWN: No.

TREAT: This is their last chance to practice and they're late.

PATTI: They'll be here.

TREAT: We only have this cabin for a half hour.

PATTI: Maybe they forgot.

TREAT: They didn't forget! How could they forget?

PATTI: *(To Treat)* Go look for them then.

TREAT: I did. They're nowhere.

PATTI: Geez, I was only kidding about the coyotes, but maybe—

TREAT: They'll just have to go on without warming up. There's no time. We're hiking to Willow Lake in an hour and Mr. Dawson said we'll be there most of the day.

(Enter OSCAR.)

PATTI: Oscar!

TREAT: Finally. Where's Beanie?

LIGHTS UP!

(OSCAR shrugs his shoulders.)

TREAT: You don't know where he is?

(OSCAR shakes his head.)

PATTI: Weren't you two together?

(OSCAR nods his head.)

TREAT: Yes, no, what?

(OSCAR hangs his head and slumps to the floor.)

PATTI: *(To Oscar)* What's wrong with you?

(OSCAR looks up and silently moves his lips They watch him.)

TREAT: Ooookay, this is weird.

(OSCAR gets up and holds his throat.)

PATTI: Ah, charades! Ok, um, throat... dying of thirst! Hanging?

TREAT: Wait a second, oh, no! NO, NO, NO!

PATTI: What, Treat?

TREAT: *(To Oscar)* You lost your voice!

(OSCAR nods his head)

TREAT: You can't speak.

(OSCAR shakes his head.)

TREAT: And if you can't speak, that means YOU CAN'T SING!

PATTI: He's just kidding.

OSCAR: (*Hoarse and scratchy*) Uh-huh.

PATTI: He's just pranking us. Ha, ha, ha, Oscar. Very funny. You guys thought this up last night. Ha, ha.

(OSCAR shakes his head.)

PATTI: You're wasting time, Oscar. Come on.

OSCAR: *(Hoarse)* It's not a prank! Ow, it hurts to talk.

TREAT: Quit messing around.

PATTI: Oscar, where's Beanie?

OSCAR: *(Hoarse)* I don't know.

PATTI: Oh, wow. Eeeek. Maybe this is for real.

OSCAR: Uh-huh.

PATTI: I don't think he's kidding. I think he really lost his voice.

OSCAR: I did.

(Enter BEANIE. His face and neck are covered in mosquito bites.)

BEANIE: Hi. *(Sees Oscar.)* So now you guys know about Oscar.

PATTI: Beanie, your face!

BEANIE: I know. It's killing me.

TREAT: It's killing us, too. WHAT HAPPENED TO YOU GUYS?!!!

BEANIE: Mine is mosquito bites. I don't know how Oscar lost his voice except it was pretty cold last night and that might not have been good for his throat.

PATTI: Why didn't you use bug spray, Beanie?

BEANIE: I put sunscreen on by mistake.

TREAT: We've got bigger problems than your swollen, bulbous face. We have to get Oscar's voice back by tonight.

BEANIE: Not gonna happen. The nurse says it's laryngitis.

PATTI: What's that?

BEANIE: It means he can't talk.

PATTI: Well, we know *that*! But for how long?

BEANIE: She said maybe a week.

TREAT: A whole week?! WHAT ABOUT THE CONTEST?!

BEANIE: I don't know.

TREAT: *(To Oscar)* This is all your fault! It's from sleeping outside. It was freezing last night. WHAT WERE YOU THINKING?!

OSCAR: *(Hoarse)* I – I , ahhhhh.

TREAT: The best voice on the planet and you go and get laryn – whatever.

PATTI: It's not Oscar's fault.

TREAT: Yes it is!

PATTI: Beanie, *you're* going to have to sing and *Oscar* can play the drum, er, pail.

(*OSCAR lets out a dramatic sob.*)

BEANIE: I can't sing!

(*OSCAR lets out another sob.*)

TREAT: Just try. Come on, you can do it.

BEANIE: I mean, look at me. I can't get up on stage with this face, even if I could sing.

PATTI: He's right. He looks disgusting. Sorry, Beanie, but you do.

TREAT: (*To Beanie*) I don't care what you look like! Sing! Just sing! SING!! We have to have two people from Grey Wolf up there tonight doing something.

OSCAR: Ohhhhhhh.

TREAT: Zip it, Oscar! Beanie, SING!

BEANIE: *(Singing very badly)* "When the night has come, and the land is dark and the moon is the only—"

PATTI: Stop!! Please! That's awful, Beanie. Sorry, but it is.

BEANIE: I told you I couldn't sing.

TREAT: Beanie, go find the rest of the Grey Wolves. Someone has to have some kind of talent.

BEANIE: I already asked everybody at breakfast. Nobody. Nada.

PATTI: Hey, guys, you know how I said I could walk with a glass of water on my head? Well, I can't, I just said that.

TREAT: So, our dream of breaking the losing streak officially ends right this minute?

BEANIE: Looks that way.

PATTI: Unlesssssss—

(PATTI turns and stares at FAWN.)

23

LIGHTS UP!

TREAT: *(To Patti)* Are you looking at *Fawn*?!!

PATTI: She's our only hope. There's no one left! Otherwise we forfeit completely.

BEANIE: At least we'd forfeit with some pride.

PATTI: Pride? Beanie, have you looked in the mirror? And look at Oscar.

TREAT: Whatever. Either way we're done for.

PATTI: Fawn, I know you're really shy and everything—but, do you think you could represent the Grey Wolf cabins with Beanie tonight? Do *something*. As you see, we are desperate.

OSCAR: *(Moaning)* Ohhhhhhhhhhh.

FAWN: Okay.

TREAT: What?

BEANIE: Huh?

PATTI: Really? You will?

FAWN: Yeah.

PATTI: Oh, my gosh, that's great!

BEANIE: Is it? Do you know what you just did, Patti?

PATTI: Yes, saved the day.

BEANIE: This is crazy.

PATTI: Thank you, Fawn!

TREAT: Wow, okay. Okay.

BEANIE: *(To Fawn) W*ait, so what is it you're gonna do—

(Suddenly there's a pounding on the door.)

TREAT: Come on, we've gotta go. The next group is here to practice. Everybody be there tonight.

Blackout

End of Scene Two

Scene Three

Later that evening. The stage area
of the dining hall. The talent
show is in progress.

FAWN, TREAT, BEANIE, PATTI
and OSCAR are in the wings.

TREAT: *(a wreck)* Okay, okay, it's gonna be fine, it's good, it's all good. We're cool. We're all here. We're on next. Okay.

PATTI: Relax, Treat. Geez.

(TREAT yanks PATTI aside so others can't hear.)

TREAT: Relax? We are about to put *Fawn* on stage. *Fawn*!! The person who never spoke until yesterday, and then all she said was "okay" and "yeah".

PATTI: Shhhh-hhh, she'll hear you.

TREAT: The person who doesn't participate in anything. What were we thinking?! What were we thinking?!

PATTI: Ah, that we had to find someone?

TREAT: We should've just forfeited. She and Beanie never practiced together. The Black Bears are gonna win anyway – their dance just now was epic. It *is* a jinx. The Grey Wolf cabin jinx. We're living it in real time. Another victim of the Grey Wolf cabin witch's spell.

PATTI: Come on, let's go, Fawn and Beanie are on next.

TREAT: She still hasn't told us what she is going to do out there. Why won't she tell us? See? She doesn't talk!

PATTI: (*To Fawn and Beanie*) You guys ready?

BEANIE: I guess.

FAWN: *(To Beanie.)* Just play the pail like before.

BEANIE: Whatever.

TREAT: *(To the duo)* Okay, go get 'em you two. *(Turns to others)* Shoot me. Shoot me now.

PATTI: Shhhhhhhhh.

(FAWN walks on stage with sudden confidence and poise. BEANIE follows her and sits on a stool next to her with the pail. FAWN takes the mic and pauses for a moment.)

FAWN: *(Into mic)* This is dedicated to anyone whoever felt different.

FAWN: *(rapping)*

Standing by the lockers
and then they try to block her,
they laugh and try to knock her,
they say she's off her rocker,
cause she's not a talker.

Ask why, big guy, bye bye, too shy,
let me by, gonna cry.

Can't have a conversation,
Forget the explanation,

Just leads to my frustration,
I'm just a small mutation.

Can't talk, won't talk, I'm airlock,
you balk, you squawk,
ad hoc, who cares?

Too bad, too shy, bye bye,
why why, let me by, gonna cry,

You're you, I'm me, makes us "we",
Let it be, you'll see,
Let's agree.

Not a talker, who cares?
put on airs
let's just share—
our differences.

*(There is thunderous applause from the audience.
OSCAR, PATTI and TREAT are dumbstruck.)*

(THEY shout from the wings.)

TREAT: Holy cow! I mean, holy cow!

PATTI: That was awesome!!!

LIGHTS UP!

OSCAR: (*scratchy voice*) Yeah!

TREAT: Way to go, Fawn! You too, Bean.

PATTI: Treat, Ms. Meadows wants you. Back there.

(*TREAT runs off stage briefly and comes back with the trophy. He walks onto the stage with the other Grey Wolves behind him.*)

TREAT: (*Into mic*) Ms. Meadows just said since we are making Camp Big Horn history tonight—

(*Applause and cheers*)

TREAT: Yep, that's right.

(*More applause.*)

TREAT: She said that I could present the trophy to the Grey Wolf Cabins. Congratulations Grey Wolves, we did it. We broke the 50-year losing streak! (*Hands FAWN the trophy*) This goes to you, Fawn. You did it.

FAWN: And Beanie.

TREAT: And Beanie.

FAWN: *(Into mic)* Thank you. I'm very proud to accept this for all the Grey Wolves.

TREAT: I just want to say that I know a lot of the kids out there are thinking this, too, but Fawn, thanks for showing us that it is important not to judge people, and that it is okay to be different.

OSCAR: *(bad scratchy voice)* That's right. And you were way awesome.

FAWN: Thank you.

PATTI: This is so exciting! Yay!!!!

BEANIE: And we broke the witch's spell.

OSCAR: *Fawn* did.

FAWN: We all did.

ALL: Yay!!! Go Grey Wolves!

Blackout
The End

SET, PROPS, COSTUMES and MAKE-UP

The Talent Show

SET PIECES
Table
Chairs
Poster on wall announcing *Camp Big Horn Annual Talent Show*

PROPS
Poster Boards -2
Markers
Trophy *
Plastic pail

*Prop Construction Tips

Trophy: Thrift stores often have an old trophy or two. Also, check DIY sites online; there are many tutorials to create one. Or, take a plastic water goblet and glue the base to an inverted jar lid and paint it gold or black.

COSTUMES
Summer camp gear.

MAKE-UP
Mosquito bites – dot lipstick all over the face; use removable glue dots painted pinkish red.

SOUND EFFECTS
Applause sound track if available.

THE RADIO GHOST

CAST OF CHARACTERS

All characters are about 10-12 years old

TRINA

MADISON

CARLOS

ZACH

IVY – a visitor from the past.

EXTRAS optional

PLACE

Hartville, a small town in Indiana.

TIME

The present, summer. *

SETTING

A garage.

* The play is set in 2021, but can be changed to reflect the current year. If so, change the radio code on page 62 to reflect that year. Ivy's year, 1921, remains the same.

THE RADIO GHOST

Trina's family garage. There is a
bike, roller blades, an old radio,
and a small TV.

AT RISE: TRINA and MADISON
are trying to fix Madison's bike.
ZACH is looking around.

TRINA: Yep, your chain came off.

MADISON: That's the second time this week -
so annoying.

TRINA: I can fix it.

MADISON: Thanks, Trina.

TRINA: (*Working on chain*) Here, hold this right
here while I straighten the chain.

ZACH: Hurry up, you guys, it might rain.

MADISON: We still have to wait for Carlos.

TRINA: (*to Zach*): You *could* help us you know.

ZACH: You're doing a fine job yourselves.

TRINA: Should we ride to Creek's Mill?

MADISON: Are you allowed to go that far? I don't think I am.

TRINA: I'm not sure. I'll ask when I get back.

MADISON: Zach, what are you doing?

ZACH: Just looking around.

TRINA: There's nothing in this garage except junk.

(*ZACH sees an old radio.*)

ZACH: What is this?

TRINA: An old radio. My mom just bought it at a garage sale.

ZACH: Cool! Does it work?

TRINA: I don't think so.

ZACH: Why would she buy it if it doesn't work?

(ZACH starts to lift the radio.)

TRINA: She bought it for her friend. Be careful!

ZACH: I just want to see if it works. It looks really old.

(ZACH examines the radio.
He turns it upside down.)

ZACH: (*Reading*) Westinghouse. Made in San Francisco. 1920. Wow.

TRINA: That's why my mom bought it. Her friend has an antique shop.

MADISON: *(Points)* You can plug it in over there.

(ZACH plugs in the radio and
fiddles with the knobs.)

ZACH: Awesome. Look, it has dials for tuning. People actually listened to this thing once.

TRINA: Well, there was no T.V. I guess they had no choice.

MADISON: No T.V. or video games. I wouldn't have survived.

ZACH: *(Fiddling)* Nothing's happening.

TRINA: Told ya.

(ZACH is still trying the radio. Enter CARLOS.)

CARLOS: Hey, what's up? You guys ready?

TRINA: We're almost done fixing Madison's chain.

CARLOS: Anybody want to ride out to Creek's Mill?

TRINA: That's what I said!

CARLOS: They have the best hills.

MADISON: I hope my bike makes it.

CARLOS: We'd better get going in case it rains.

MADISON: I don't want to get stuck at Creek's Mill in the rain.

TRINA: It's not going to rain.

MADISON: How do you know?

TRINA: I just know.

CARLOS: *(Referring to radio)* What's that, Zach?

ZACH: An old radio.

CARLOS: Let me see.

ZACH: I can't get it to work.

CARLOS: Bang on it.

TRINA: No, don't! Leave it. Let's just go.

CARLOS: Oh, snap, I forgot my helmet. I'll be right back.

(CARLOS exits.)

(ZACH is still fussing with the radio. There is a loud buzzing and static noise.)

ZACH: Hey, listen, something's happening! Do you hear that?

MADISON: I hear scratching noises.

ZACH: That's static. This is so cool! It works.

(ZACH turns the dial.)

MADISON: There's no music or anything.

(Suddenly a voice is heard, apparently from the radio.)

VOICE (IVY): Hello.

ZACH: Hey, I found a station.

VOICE (IVY): Hello? Is somebody there?

TRINA: It does work!

ZACH: This is awesome.

VOICE (IVY): Can you hear me?

MADISON: Are they talking to *us*?

ZACH: No. You can't talk back and forth on this.

MADISON: It must be a radio show then.

VOICE (IVY): Hello, can you hear me?

TRINA: I don't know. It sure sounds like they're trying to talk to us.

ZACH: Nah.

VOICE (IVY): Hello. I can hear you. Can you hear me?

MADISON: Huh?! What kind of radio is that?

VOICE (IVY): Hello.

ZACH: I – I —this is weird.

TRINA: Say something else, Zach.

ZACH: *(Loudly)* TESTING, TESTING, 1,2,3. IS ANYBODY THERE?

MADISON: YO! CAN YOU HEAR US?

(While the three are huddled around the radio, IVY walks in behind them. She is dressed in clothes from the early 1920's.)

IVY: Hello.

(They turn around and jump back.)

MADISON: Ahhhhhhhh!!

TRINA: Who...who...are you?

IVY: Ivy Matthews.

ZACH: Were you...uh...just talking to us through the radio?

IVY: Golly wombats! I think so, yes! I could hear you.

TRINA: But how?

IVY: I don't know.

ZACH: Oooookay.

MADISON: How did you get here?

IVY: I was turning the dial on our radio and the next thing I knew I – I - felt a strange force, like something pulling me. That's all I remember.

ZACH: That's so trippy.

TRINA: Where do you live?

IVY: San Francisco.

ZACH: Like in California?

IVY: Yes, like you.

ZACH: We're not in California. We're in Hartville, Indiana, the most boring city on the planet.

IVY: You're playing a game with me.

MADISON: Oh, I am sooooooo freaked out right now!!!! Ahhhhhhhhh.

TRINA: Calm down, Madison.

MADISON: Calm down? That girl just came out of a radio from California.

ZACH: She didn't come out of the radio. We were looking right at the radio when she walked in from over there.

IVY: He's right. Somehow I just arrived here.

MADISON: But how?

IVY: *(Confused)* I don't know. I turned on the radio after my lessons today and, well, now I am standing here –

ZACH: In Trina's garage in Hartville, Indiana.

MADISON: Ohhhh, make her go awayyyy.

LIGHTS UP!

(Enter CARLOS.)

CARLOS: Okay, I'm back. Let's go, guys. *(sees Ivy)* Oh, hi.

IVY: Hello.

CARLOS: Are you Trina's cousin?

TRINA: This is Ivy.

MADISON: From "San Francisco".

CARLOS: Huh?

TRINA: Zach brought Ivy here –

MADISON: By voodoo magic. Get out while you can.

CARLOS: What?

MADISON: Crazy, right?

CARLOS: *(To Ivy)* Are you riding to Creek's Mill with us? Did you bring your bike?

IVY: Bicycle? No.

MADISON: Hello, am I the only sane person here?! Even her clothes are different. Old-fashioned like.

TRINA: They are.

ZACH: Oh, man! Oh, man, you've got to be kidding!

TRINA: What, Zach?

ZACH: I saw this in a movie once. Ivy, what year is it?

IVY: 1921.

MADISON: Huh?

TRINA: It's 2021, not 1921.

IVY: Don't tease me. It's not nice.

ZACH: We're not teasing you.

MADISON: No, *you're* teasing us.

CARLOS: Are you—like—a ghost?

IVY: Of course not. What a strange question.

TRINA: More like a time traveler.

ZACH: That's what I'm talking about: time traveler!

(CARLOS points to a small TV)

CARLOS: Do you know what this is?

IVY: No.

CARLOS: A television.

IVY: I've never heard of it, or saw one.

TRINA: I have an idea. I'll be right back.

(TRINA rushes out. Madison holds up roller blades.)

MADISON: How about these?

IVY: Are those ice skates?

MADISON: No.

ZACH: You've never seen these before?

IVY: No.

MADISON: *(Doubtful)* You've never seen roller blades?

CARLOS: What about this bicycle?

IVY: I know what a bicycle is! But I've never seen a bicycle with such bright colors.

(TRINA runs back in with a laptop.)

TRINA: Okay. Here. Do you know what this is?

IVY: No.

(TRINA opens it up and shows her.)

TRINA: It's a computer. There's YouTube, Google, video games.

IVY: I don't understand what you just said.

MADISON: She's just messing with us. (*To Ivy*) There's no way you are from 1921 because if you were, you'd be, like a hundred years old.

ZACH: Not if she time traveled. It's in another dimension. People exist at the same time. That's so cool. I want to do that, too. I want to get out of here and go back in time.

CARLOS: You're crazy. You can't do that.

MADISON: Anyone can pretend to not know what this stuff is.

IVY: I'm not pretending!

MADISON: Let's go ride to Creek's Mill and when we get back she will be gone.

CARLOS: We're not going anyway. Look outside.

ZACH: Rain! I told you it was gonna rain.

(IVY starts to cry.)

IVY: Why are you being so unkind? I'm Ivy Matthews. I live at 135 Mission Street, San Francisco, California. My parents are Edwin and Victoria Matthews. I have two younger brothers, Walter and James.

(They all stare at her and realize IVY is telling the truth. There's a pause while this sinks in.)

CARLOS: Oh, wow.

TRINA: I think this might really be happening.

ZACH: Yeah.

MADISON: No way.

TRINA: We're sorry, Ivy. This is just really weird. You lived, *live*, like–a hundred years ago.

CARLOS: Yeah, it's not every day we meet a real live zombie.

TRINA: Carlos!

CARLOS: Ghost.

TRINA: Time traveler!

ZACH: Are you hungry?

IVY: I am. I didn't eat my noon meal. Instead I came—here—

TRINA: I'll get you something.

(TRINA exits.)

CARLOS: You want to see T.V.? The thing you never saw before?

(CARLOS turns on T.V. IVY is fascinated.)

IVY: Moving pictures in that little box! And they talk!

ZACH: Yeah.

IVY: Golly wombats.

MADISON: Maybe we should call her parents.

ZACH: We can't if they're in another dimension.

MADISON: Stop! Even if that was true, which I don't think it is, we could still call her parents. They had phones back then, didn't they?

IVY: Phones?

MADISON: Telephones.

IVY: Yes, but we don't have one.

(CARLOS has been looking at the laptop.)

ZACH: How are you going to get back home?

IVY: I don't know.

ZACH: Maybe I could go back with you.

IVY: If you want.

CARLOS: You're crazy, Zach. You can't do that.

ZACH: It would be so cool to go back in time.

CARLOS: Don't you think your family would miss you?

ZACH: I'd come back.

CARLOS: Maybe you couldn't.

(TRINA returns with a small sandwich.)

TRINA: Here you go.

IVY: Thank you.

(IVY bites into the sandwich.)

TRINA: It's peanut butter and jelly.

IVY: This is delicious! I've never tasted anything so good.

MADISON: You've never had peanut butter and jelly?

(CARLOS still looking at laptop.)

CARLOS: *(Reading from computer)* It says PB&J sandwiches weren't popular till the 1940s.

ZACH: Who knew.

TRINA: We have to figure out how to get you back home, Ivy. You know, to 1921. To San Francisco.

IVY: Oh, yes, please do.

MADISON: This girl is NOT from 1921 because that is impossible! Sorry, Ivy. Maybe you hit your head or something and wandered into the garage. Maybe you *think* that is what happened to you, but you did not travel through "radio waves" and come here.

ZACH: Maybe she did, Madison. There's a lot we don't know about the universe.

CARLOS: (*Still on laptop*) Who's the president, Ivy?

IVY: Warren Harding.

CARLOS: (*Looking*) That's right!

CARLOS: Vice-president?

IVY: Calvin Coolidge.

CARLOS: How many states are there?

IVY: Forty-eight, silly. Everyone knows that.

ZACH: Wow.

TRINA: Holy moly.

MADISON: So, she learned it in school like we did.

CARLOS: Did you know who the president and vice president were in 1921, Madison?

MADISON: It still doesn't prove anything.

IVY: Do you think I could have another sandwich please?

TRINA: Oh, sure, okay. I'll be right back.

(TRINA exits.)

IVY: Could I take a train home?

CARLOS: It doesn't work like that. You'd still be in 2021.

ZACH: In that story I read, the person has to leave the same way they came.

CARLOS: Through the radio?

ZACH: If Ivy is sure that's how it happened.

IVY: All I know is I want to go home.

MADISON: I have an idea. When it stops raining, let's walk up and down the street and see if anyone recognizes her, or she recognizes her house.

CARLOS: We know every house and family around here, Madison. Obviously she isn't from here.

MADISON: It's worth a try.

ZACH: Madison's right, we have nothing to lose.

CARLOS: *(Looking)* It's almost stopped raining.

(TRINA enters with another sandwich and hands it to IVY.)

TRINA: Here you go.

MADISON: Bring the sandwich with you, Ivy. We're going to find where you live. Come on, everybody.

IVY: I live at 135 Mission Street, San Francisco California.

MADISON: I know, I know. You already told us.

ZACH: If this doesn't work, then she can try going back through the radio.

(They all exit.)

IVY *(off stage, on exit):* Oh, golly wombats! Look at all the automobiles!! And so many kinds!

Blackout

End of Scene One

Scene Two

Later that day.
The stage is empty as
THEY all file in, tired and
defeated.

CARLOS: Well, so much for that.

ZACH: We walked like ten miles.

TRINA: Ten blocks anyway.

MADISON: I thought for sure somebody would recognize her.

TRINA: No one.

IVY: My stomach hurts.

MADISON: No kidding. You ate four peanut butter and jelly sandwiches.

IVY: Four?

TRINA: Yeah, two from here.

CARLOS: One from my house.

ZACH: And one from mine.

TRINA: Well, since that search didn't work, what now?

CARLOS: We try what Zach said: leave the way she came.

IVY: Yes, let's try. Please.

CARLOS: *(Looking around)* Where's the radio?

ZACH: *(Points)* Right over there.

CARLOS: No, it's not.

TRINA: It's gone! The radio is gone!

ZACH: What?! It was right there when we left.

TRINA: Oh, no! My mom was going to take it to mail to her friend in New York.

CARLOS: See if she's still home.

TRINA: *(Looks out)* Her car's gone!

ZACH: Great.

CARLOS: *(Looking at door to house)* There's a note here from your mom, Trina.

(They rush to the note.)

TRINA *(Reading)* "I ran to the store to get a shipping box, then stopping by Grandma's. I won't be long."

ZACH: Maybe the radio's in the house.

(TRINA rushes out of garage.)

MADISON: And if the radio is gone, then what?

ZACH: I don't know.

MADISON: We're going to have to tell our parents.

CARLOS: Yeah, Madison is right. She can't live in Trina's garage forever.

IVY: I want to go home!

CARLOS: We're trying, Ivy.

(Enter TRINA carrying the radio.)

ZACH: Yesssss!

TRINA: We have to hurry, before my mom gets back.

(They all huddle around the radio, fiddling with the dials.)

ZACH: I've made up my mind: I'm gonna try to leave too.

TRINA: No computers. No TV.

CARLOS: No cell phones.

TRINA: No family. No home.

ZACH: Yeah, I know, but—

TRINA: But what, Zach? If you go, you might not be able to get back.

ZACH: Well...

TRINA: Let's just try to get Ivy back first, could we?

CARLOS: Ready, Ivy?

IVY: Ready. But what do I do?

TRINA: Just think about going home.

LIGHTS UP!

*(IVY closes her eyes. ALL wait.
Nothing happens.)*

ZACH: Nothing's happening. Concentrate, Ivy.

IVY: I am.

TRINA: Maybe there's a special word or code.

MADISON: Yeah, the word is prank.

TRINA: Madison, will you quit? Ivy, did you say something when you...traveled here?

IVY: All I said was hello, hello, can you hear me?

CARLOS: There's got to be something else you did.

IVY: What if it was a one-way ticket? Oh, I'll never see my family again!

ZACH: Ivy, do you remember what number you turned to on your radio dial?

IVY: Yes, I was trying to find some music which is 20 and 21. I don't know if I went past those numbers. I can't remember.

TRINA: Zach, what number was this on when Ivy showed up? Do you know?

ZACH: (*Looks*) It's on 21 now. The static started when I hit 19. I remember.

CARLOS: Wait a second, if it's stopped on 21 and you heard noise at 19—

TRINA: 1921!

CARLOS: Like a combination lock.

TRINA: And that's when Ivy showed up.

IVY: I turned mine to 20. Then 21.

ZACH: 2021!

MADISON: Ahhhhhhhhh!! That's this year!

TRINA: And the radio was made in San Francisco!

ZACH: So, if Ivy's radio at home is still on the last station before she left—

IVY: Then I can go home!

TRINA: If this works.

IVY: If it does, I want to thank you for this day. I will never forget you. Or the peanut butter and jelly sandwiches.

TRINA: Good bye, Ivy.

CARLOS: Good luck.

ZACH: Have a safe trip.

MADISON: Adios.

(*ALL huddle around the radio. ZACH tunes in.*)

IVY: That's my mother's voice! Mama!

TRINA: I don't hear anything.

CARLOS: Me either.

MADISON: There's no voice.

IVY: Can't you hear it? Mama, I'm here!

(*IVY has crossed to behind the radio while others remain huddled in front of it.*)

ZACH: (*Turning dial*) Okay, here it goes: 19...and 21.

CARLOS: If we're right, that's the code and should take her back.

(ALL stand and wait with their eyes closed.)

MADISON: (*Opening eyes*) Nothing happened.

ZACH: Snap!

TRINA: No? Then where's Ivy?

(IVY is gone.)

CARLOS: She's gone!

ZACH: Oh, man!!!! I don't believe it!

TRINA: Did that just really happen?

MADISON: I think it did!

CARLOS: It worked. It actually worked.

MADISON: Ahhhhhhhhh!!!

TRINA: It's okay, Madison.

(CARLOS looks all around the garage and out the door.)

CARLOS: Maybe she just got as far as the front yard.

(TRINA looks around.)

TRINA: Yeah, or the street or something.

CARLOS: I don't see her.

TRINA: She's gone.

CARLOS: We have to tell everybody about this.

TRINA: Or not. Who'd believe us?

ZACH: Yeah, I can hardly believe it.

TRINA: Do you still want to go, too, Zach?

ZACH: No. I guess my time is with you guys. Here and now. Plus, I don't want to go anywhere that doesn't have peanut butter and jelly sandwiches yet.

TRINA: So, Madison, you never believed Ivy.

MADISON: I was so sure she was pranking us. I mean, come on, who would believe that crazy story?

CARLOS: Us.

TRINA: Yeah, we did.

MADISON: True.

ZACH: What do you say now, Madison?

MADISON: I say—golly wombats!

(ALL laugh as lights fade.)

Blackout

The End

SET, PROPS, SOUND
and COSTUMES

The Radio Ghost

SET PIECES

Garage items: Anything available to give appearance of a garage: paint cans, rakes, etc.

Small TV *

Bicycle

Old radio *

Table or desk for the radio. If using a table, cover with a tablecloth that reaches floor.

*Set Construction Tips

TV: Cardboard box construction is fine. Screen faces upstage so audience will not see.

Radio: Two shoe boxes can be glued together and painted; or cardboard box painted.

PROPS

Roller Blades

Note from Mom to tape on door laptop *

Peanut butter and jelly sandwiches (two) *

Bicycle

*Prop Construction Tips

Laptop: cardboard construction.

PB&J sandwiches: use soft bread, no crusts, no peanut butter— it's too difficult to eat on stage. Instead serve bread with a little butter or mayo. Serve small halves only so the actor playing Ivy has time to finish eating. Water optional.

COSTUMES

Ivy: 1920s style dress or skirt and blouse. No pants. Shoes should be flats or ballet slippers. Daily wear for the rest of cast.

SOUND

Static and buzzing noises from radio: sound app if available.

IVY'S DISAPPEARANCE AT THE END

If you have a small desk available, turn it around so the back of the desk is facing the audience. The radio will sit on it. At the moment of sending Ivy back in time, have all characters, except Ivy, stand, huddled around the radio with their backs to the audience (the rare occasion I recommend actors' backs to the audience). Ivy will stand behind the desk, facing the audience. The standing huddled group will then, hopefully, mask her departure as she quickly ducks down and into the empty space below. The same technique applies to using a table with a cover to the floor, leaving an opening in back so that Ivy can quickly duck into the space as she "disappears." Or, Ivy can simply walk off stage the same way she entered, and the kids, so focused on the radio, do not see her leave, and then realize she is nowhere to be found.

THE GREAT POTATO TRIAL

CAST OF CHARACTERS

JUDGE – a turnip.

RUSSET – Russet potato and plaintiff.

SWEET YAM – sweet potato and defendant.

CELERIA STALK – celery/ Ms. Yam's lawyer.

BROCK A. LEE – broccoli/ Russet's lawyer.

BUTTERNUT – butternut squash.

ZEA MAIZE – corn on the cob.

CAB BIDGE – cabbage head.

HEIR LOOM – sweet potato.

PLACE

Veggie Run – a vegetable farming community

SETTING

A courtroom.

THE GREAT POTATO TRIAL

A courtroom in the farming town
of Veggie Run.

AT RISE: JUDGE is seated at the
desk. Downstage right sits
SWEET YAM and her attorney,
CELERIA STALK. Stage left is
BROCK A. LEE.

Any witnesses and spectators sit
in other seats.

JUDGE: Mr. Lee, where is your client, Mr.
Russet Potato? We are about to begin the trial.

BROCK: I'm sorry, your honor. I don't know
what's keeping him. It's not like him to be late.

JUDGE: If he doesn't show up in the next two
minutes, this case will be dismissed. We all
have things to do. He's the one who brought

this complaint to the court in the first place, so I should think he would be on time.

STALK: I move we dismiss.

YAM: I second that.

JUDGE: Quiet, Ms. Yam. You are not allowed to chime in. You are, may I remind you, the accused?

YAM: The wrongly accused.

JUDGE: That is yet to be decided.

(Enter MR. RUSSET, out of breath.)

RUSSET: I'm here, I'm here, sorry, your honor.

STALK: It's about time you got here, potato head.

RUSSET: I got stuck behind a tomato truck.

JUDGE: Tomatoes. Yuk. I can't stand tomatoes. All right, come on, everyone, let us begin.

RUSSET: All set, your honor.

JUDGE: The court of Veggie Run will now hear the case of *Russet Potatoes versus Sweet Potatoes*, or Yams, as they are also known.

STALK: (*Jumps up*) Yams are NOT sweet potatoes, your honor! It's a common mistake, but for the record my client is a sweet potato, not a yam.

JUDGE: Same difference.

(There's a gasp from the CROWD.)

STALK: They are not the same. Yams are *not* grown here, sir. Yams are grown in Asia and Africa. It's a common mistake but one that is important to my client. They are different potatoes. Yams have yellow flesh; sweet potatoes, dark orange flesh.

JUDGE: But even your client's last name is *Yam*.

STALK: Her last name is Yam due to some confusion in a shipping yard many years ago.

JUDGE: All right. *Russet Potatoes versus Sweet Potatoes*. Let's get on with it.

BROCK: We will show the court that the sweet potatoes of Veggie Run, under their leader, Ms. Yam, are trying to take over the Russet potato business by destroying all the Russet potato crops. There is now barely one yellow Russet potato left in the field, save my client here. This was all done on the night of September 20th.

(RUSSET sniffles, dabbing his eyes.)

STALK: My client denies all charges.

BROCK: You will hear from witnesses today who will tell you they saw Ms. Yam, along with her buds, in the north field, in the dark of night, digging up the yellow Russets and disposing of the crop.

JUDGE: Disposing of them where?

BROCK: They have not yet been found.

JUDGE: What reason would the sweet potatoes have to destroy the popular and delicious Russet potato?

BROCK: You just said it yourself! Popular and delicious. By destroying the regular potato crop, restaurants in the area are now forced to switch to sweet potatoes in place of the yellow ones. And the reason for this crime? One of the oldest on record: jealousy.

STALK: That's ridiculous. My client and the sweet potatoes were nowhere near the north field that night. And how do you know that whoever dug up the potatoes was trying to take over the potato business? Maybe they just like Russet potatoes!

BROCK: It will soon be obvious.

JUDGE: Carry on, Brock.

BROCK: As Mr. Russet stated in his written report, there were shreds of orange pulp left at the scene. No doubt when the poor Russets tried to fend off their attackers.

(RUSSET lets out a sob.)

JUDGE: Get a hold of yourself, Russet.

RUSSET: Yes, your honor.

BROCK: I submit this sample as Exhibit A. Clearly from sweet potatoes.

> *(BROCK hands over a bag*
> *of shredded orange pulp.)*

JUDGE: (*Looking*) It's orange, all right. Yep, dark orange.

STALK: Your honor, do you mind? You are not supposed to take sides.

JUDGE: I just said it's orange. Geez.

STALK: Let the record show that I went to the potato field this morning and examined the orange residue myself. And I can tell you there is no proof that the orange residue is that of a sweet potato.

BROCK: The question is, how and why would there be this dark orange flesh found among the Russets on the night in question? Russets, who have a pale, yellow-white flesh?

JUDGE: All right. Ms. Stalk, please bring up your first witness.

STALK: I call Mr. Heir Loom to the stand.

(HEIR LOOM, a sweet potato, comes up.)

STALK: Mr. Loom, state your name and field.

HEIR LOOM: Heir Loom, west field.

STALK: You are a sweet potato, correct?

HEIR LOOM: I am.

STALK: And you grow in the same field as all the varieties of sweet potatoes, do you not?

HEIR LOOM: Yes, we all live there together.

STALK: And can you tell us where you were on the night of September 20th?

HEIR LOOM: At home in my field, along with all the other sweet potatoes.

STALK: Did you see any sweet potatoes, namely Ms. Yam here, get up and leave at any time?

HEIR LOOM: No, I did not.

STALK: Would you have heard if a group of sweet potatoes had gotten up and left the field?

HEIR LOOM: Yes, I would have. I am a very light sleeper. I know all that goes on in my field, and I saw no one leave that night.

STALK: That's all, thank you.

(BROCK approaches.)

BROCK: Mr. Loom, your variety of sweet potato goes by another name, too, doesn't it?

HEIR LOOM: Sometimes.

BROCK: And what is that name?

HEIR LOOM: Envy.

BROCK: Envy. As in jealous.

STALK: Objection! He's picking on the witness's name.

BROCK: Isn't it true, Mr. Loom, or Mr. Envy, that you are close friends with all the sweet potatoes?

HEIR LOOM: Yes. We're a true team. We are a strong and hardy potato, originally from South America, dating back 5,000 years.

BROCK: Since you are all such good friends, wouldn't you also be willing to NOT turn in one of your own to the vegetable police, even if you knew that Sweet Yam here was guilty?

HEIR LOOM: Absolutely not! I am a sweet potato of the highest integrity and always do the right thing.

BROCK: No further questions.

JUDGE: Next witness.

BROCK: Would Cab Bidge please take the stand?

(CAB BIDGE comes up and is seated.)

CAB: Sure will.

BROCK: State your name and address.

CAB: Cab Bidge, Oak Tree Farm.

BROCK: Can you tell us what you recently discovered at the Oak Tree Café in your village?

CAB: Yes. There is a sign out front that states the only French fries available are sweet potato fries and the only mashed potatoes are mashed yams. Err, mashed sweet potatoes. I can never tell yams and sweet potatoes apart.

(A gasp from the CROWD at this.)

BROCK: And, did you ask why they were serving this replacement?

CAB: I did. They said it was because there were no Russet potatoes available from Veggie Run, so they had to use sweet potatoes, which were plentiful. They said although it was their second choice, sweet potatoes were better than nothing.

YAM: *(Jumps up)* Better than nothing?! We're delicious! What do you think people eat at Thanksgiving? Sweet potatoes smothered in butter, then baked with tiny marshmallows, that's what.

JUDGE: Silence, Ms. Yam! It is not your turn to talk.

BROCK: Continue, Bidge.

CAB: I asked why there were no yellow Russets available and they said they heard the Russets got dug up and hidden somewhere.

STALK: Objection! This is hearsay. He's no witness. *Hearing* about it is not the same as *seeing* a crime in action.

BROCK: I have nothing further, your honor.

(STALK approaches.)

STALK: Mr. Bidge, for the record, you never actually *saw* any potatoes being dug up and hauled away, correct?

CAB: True, but—

STALK: That will be all. Thank you.

CAB: But I think it's obvious what the sweet potatoes are doing.

STALK: We are not interested in your opinion, Mr. Bidge, just facts.

(*CAB steps down.*)

JUDGE: Who's next?

STALK: I call Butternut Squash to the stand.

BUTTERNUT: All righty! Yay! Thank you!!

(*BUTTERNUT SQUASH takes the stand.*)

STALK: Butternut, can you tell me where you and the other squash grow?

BUTTERNUT: In the south field, next to the big red barn.

STALK: And what other crops are grown in the south field?

BUTTERNUT: Green beans, peas.

STALK: And?

BUTTERNUT: Corn, zucchini.

STALK: Uh-huh. And where were you on the night of September 20th?

BUTTERNUT: In my field, enjoying the night air along with the other squash.

STALK: Do you enjoy being a butternut squash, Butternut?

BROCK: Objection! Who cares if she likes being a squash?

JUDGE: You may answer, Butternut.

BUTTERNUT: Sure, of course. Who doesn't like butternut squash?

STALK: Lots of people, actually.

BUTTERNUT: Nuh-uh.

STALK: Would you say you are as popular as the potato?

BUTTERNUT: Well, no, but—

BROCK: Objection!

JUDGE: Move on Ms. Stalk.

STALK: That will be all then, thank you.

(BUTTERNUT steps down, but then returns.)

BUTTERNUT: You're wrong, Ms. Stalk! Lots of people like butternut squash. We're very versatile.

JUDGE: *(Doubtful)* Are you really though?

BUTTERNUT: We can be baked, sautéed with butter and cinnamon, used in soups.

JUDGE: Please take your seat, Butternut.

BROCK: Will Zea Maize please take the stand.

(ZEA MAIZE comes up.)

BROCK: State your name and location.

MAIZE: Zea Maize. I live in the south field. You know, the corn fields.

BROCK: Where were you on the evening of September 20th?

MAIZE: Taking a walk under the beautiful moonlight.

BROCK: In the south field?

MAIZE: No, in the north field.

BROCK: That's quite a distance from your own area.

MAIZE: I—had trouble sleeping that night— so I walked up to the north field to tire myself out.

BROCK: Makes sense. And what did you observe while you were there?

MAIZE: I saw Ms. Yam and the other sweet potatoes digging up the Russet potatoes.

YAM: That's a lie!

JUDGE: Order in the court!

BROCK: Thank you, Ms. Maize. That is all.

(STALK approaches holding a booklet.)

STALK: Ms. Maize, you said you were walking in the moonlight?

MAIZE: Correct.

STALK: Well, according to the Farmer's Almanac here, it was a moon*less* light on September 20th, almost no light at all in any of the fields.

MAIZE: Was it? I hadn't noticed.

STALK: If there was no moonlight, how could you have seen that it was the sweet potatoes tearing up the field?

MAIZE: Well, uh, I couldn't see that well, but, uh, I could make out the sweet potato's shape in the shadows.

STALK: The shape? So, you just *assumed* it was Ms. Yam and her buds. Couldn't it just as easily have been another vegetable you saw taking the Russets? Turnips? Rutabagas?

MAIZE: Maybe.

STALK: What did you do after that?

MAIZE: I ran back to the corn fields.

STALK: Did you report what you saw?

MAIZE: No, I went to sleep.

STALK: Did you hear any suspicious noises or activity after you returned home?

MAIZE: Why would I? I told you, I went to sleep. I didn't hear any noises or anything coming from the barn.

STALK: Who said anything about the barn?

MAIZE: *You* did. You just asked if I heard any noises coming from the barn.

STALK: I never said the word *barn*.

MAIZE: I - I thought you did.

BROCK: Objection. Who cares if Maize heard anything going on? It's a farm? Of course there would be noise coming from the barn—from horses, chickens.

JUDGE: Continue, Ms. Stalk.

STALK: The truth is, Ms. Maize, I believe you did hear unusual noises coming from the barn late that night, and went to see what it was, didn't you?

BROCK: Badgering the witness!

STALK: Why else would you have mentioned the *barn* when I did not?

MAIZE: (*Upset*) I don't know.

STALK: What was in the barn, Zea Maize?

MAIZE: I – I —oh, I can't do this.

STALK: Do what?

MAIZE: Lie. I can't! I did see something.

BUTTERNUT: (*Yelling*) Stop, Maizy! You didn't hear or see anything!

JUDGE: Order! Order!

MAIZE: Sorry, Butternut. I should never have said I would lie for you.

BUTTERNUT: You promised!

STALK: What did you see in the barn, Ms. Maize?

MAIZE: I – I – saw Butternut and some other butternut squash hiding the Russet potatoes in the hay loft.

LIGHTS UP!

(A loud gasp from the crowd.)

RUSSET: What?! You mean I've been wiped out by a bunch of squash?!

YAM: Butternut?! How could you?

STALK: I call Butternut Squash back to the stand.

(BUTTERNUT comes up.)

JUDGE: You may step down, Ms. Maize.

MAIZE: Thank you.

STALK: Ms. Squash—

BUTTERNUT: Okay, yes, I did it!! I did it, okay?!

STALK: But why?

YAM: Good question. Why, Butternut?

STALK: And why involve Zea Maize in your web of deceit?

BUTTERNUT: Isn't it obvious?

RUSSET, YAM, BROCK and JUDGE: No!!

BUTTERNUT: Everyone loves the Russet and other yellow and white potatoes soooo much. People even like sweet potatoes enough to make fries out of them. What about us squash? Especially us Butternuts. We're barely on the shelves except in autumn. Russets are there all year long.

(RUSSET has walked over to BUTTERNUT.)

RUSSET: And how lucky you are.

BUTTERNUT: Huh?

RUSSET: You get months off to seed in cozy pots by the window, relax in the sun, nothing to do until your busy season. We *never* get down time. Ever. We're either growing outside or growing in green houses. The demand for our potatoes never ends.

JUDGE: That's true. There's French fries, steak fries, hash browns–

STALK: Mashed, baked, tater tots, potato salad.

BROCK: Potato chips! Rippled, baked, barbecued.

STALK: Potato pancakes.

RUSSET: Potato dumplings.

BROCK: Potato soup.

RUSSET: Nobody ever asks us if we'd like a break.

BUTTERNUT: I never thought about it like that.

YAM: We sweet potatoes have the same problem as you, Butternut. We have to hear about those fabulous potato dishes all the time.

BROCK: Try being me, why don't you? Do you know how many kids hate broccoli?

JUDGE: Or a turnip! I mean, come on. People run from turnips.

BROCK: We all have a part to play in the vegetable kingdom, Butternut. And each of us is important in our own way. Together we provide everything needed for a well- balanced veggie world.

JUDGE: Even tomatoes.

ALL OTHERS: Tomatoes are a fruit!!!

JUDGE: All right, all right.

BUTTERNUT: I'm sorry, Russ. I shouldn't have done that. And Maizy told me to put the Russets back when she saw them, that it was wrong. But it was too late to move them all.

RUSSET: It's all right. No harm done. It sounds like my taters are safe in the hay.

BUTTERNUT: They are. We hid them pretty good.

RUSSET: Ms. Yam, I owe you an apology. I thought you were jealous of our success and set out to destroy us.

YAM: Well, maybe I am a little jealous, but I would never bring you and your potatoes harm.

BROCK: (*To Stalk*) You knew it was Butternut, didn't you?

STALK: I was pretty sure once I went out to the field and looked.

JUDGE: Since the Russet potatoes are okay, and if everyone here agrees to never do anything like this again, I think we can dismiss all charges today. What do you all say?

ALL: (*ad libs*) Promise, yes, okay.

JUDGE: Good. Now, let's go eat. All this talk has made me hungry.

BROCK: What are you going to have for lunch, Judge?

JUDGE: Anything but tomatoes.

(THEY all laugh.)

Blackout
The End

SET, PROPS AND COSTUMES

The Great Potato Trial

SET PIECES

Table for judge

Chairs: nine, more if using extras

PROPS

Gavel *

Farmer's Almanac *

Bag of Shredded orange pulp *

*Prop Construction Tips

Gavel: Kitchen meat tenderizer; Tinker Toys (yes, they still make them!); toy hammer.

Orange pulp: Shredded orange paper; sponge.

Farmer's Almanac: Thrift stores have old books and magazines, or design your own cover and glue to a small magazine or old book.

COSTUMES
Turnip
Russet Potato
Sweet Potato
Heirloom Sweet Potato
Celery
Broccoli
Butternut Squash
Cabbage
Corn on the Cob

Full costumes aren't necessary. Characters should, though, be dressed in clothes the color of their vegetable. Colored wigs and hair are always fun. You can use construction paper to make crazy kinds of headgear. I would suggest avoiding face paint which can be messy and distracting. Here is a great opportunity to get creative – have a blast!

HAPPY BIRTHDAY, BONNIE MACDOUGALL

CAST OF CHARACTERS

LISA WARNER—8 or 9 years old, Mike's sister.

MIKE WARNER—10-12 years old, Lisa's brother.

ROCCO—10-12 years old, a friend.

BELLE— 8-10 years old, a friend.

PLACE
A city in the U.S.A.

TIME
The present.

SETTING
The Warner family attic.

HAPPY BIRTHDAY, BONNIE MACDOUGAL

> An attic filled with typical attic items. There are some boxes of old dishes marked "Glass/Fragile".

> A door presumably leads down to Mike's bedroom.

> AT RISE: MIKE and his sister, LISA, are standing near the steps.

MIKE: (*Yelling down*) Yeah, Ma, I'm in my room. I know, the attic's off limits, lots of old dishes up there. Okay.

LISA: Oh, my gosh, you totally just lied to Mom.

MIKE: Not exactly

LISA: A big fat lie.

MIKE: Well, I *was* in my room.

LISA: You're not now.

MIKE: And who's in the attic with me? Hmmm, you sure look a lot like my sister.

LISA: I only came up here because you did.

MIKE: So, I didn't twist your arm. And don't even think about telling on me because I have more dirt on you than a landfill.

LISA: You do not.

MIKE: Think again, little Lisa.

LISA: Okay, but there's nothing up here anyway.

MIKE: That's what you think.

LISA: You found something?

MIKE: Yesterday.

LISA: Yesterday? You were up here before? What a sneak!

MIKE: Nothing broke.

LISA: That's not the point.

MIKE: Do you want to see what I found or not?

LISA: Show me.

MIKE: It's over here.

(MIKE leads LISA to a big box with a lid. He opens it. LISA looks.)

LISA: What is this?

MIKE: Check it out.

LISA: Are those for us?

(MIKE pulls out three gifts, beautifully wrapped, from the box.)

MIKE: No, they're for Bonnie MacDougall.

LISA: Who's Bonnie MacDougall?

MIKE: I don't know. Feel this one, shake it.

(LISA takes box and shakes it.)

LISA: What are these doing here?

MIKE: I don't know, but look, they're numbered in what order to open them.

LISA: One, two, three. "To Bonnie MacDougall". Let's ask Mom.

MIKE: Right, ask Mom so she'll know we were up here.

LISA: Good point.

MIKE: I found this, too. Look.

(MIKE hands LISA a note. She reads it aloud.)

LISA: "Dear Bonnie, we can't wait to see you. We have your birthday presents, very special gifts that I know will surprise you. They are wrapped and waiting for your arrival, as long as it takes. Signed, Your family, the Warners." Family? Our family?

MIKE: It says: "Your family, the Warners."

LISA: Wow. I wonder when she's coming.

MIKE: Look at the date; that was two years ago.

(Enter ROCCO. He sneaks up behind the two.)

ROCCO: Boo!

(MIKE and LISA jump.)

LISA: Geeeez, Rocco!

MIKE: How did you get in here?

ROCCO: Same way you did. Your mom said you were in your room but I couldn't find you, so I started looking around.

LISA: Like going through all our rooms?

ROCCO: Uh, yeah. So, what are you guys doing up here anyway?

LISA: Mike's snooping.

MIKE: *(To Rocco)* You didn't shut the door all the way, did you?

ROCCO: I don't think so.

MIKE: It sticks if you shut it all the way.

ROCCO: So what are you guys looking at?

(Off stage we hear BELLE'S voice.)

BELLE: *(off stage)* Rocco? Where did you guys go? Hey Rocco!!!

MIKE: Belle, we're up here.

BELLE: Mike? Lisa?

MIKE: (*To Rocco*) Hurry, go tell her to be quiet.

ROCCO: Why?

MIKE: Just get her, will ya?

(*ROCCO runs to stairs.*)

ROCCO: Belle, we're up here.

BELLE: (*still off stage*) Where?

MIKE: Never mind. I'll get her.

(*MIKE exits downstairs.*)

ROCCO: Ohh, digging into birthday presents early, huh?

LISA: Birthday presents, but not ours.

ROCCO: Whose?

LISA: That's what we're trying to figure out.

(*ROCCO reads the tags on the boxes.*)

ROCCO: They belong to Bonnie MacDougall.

LISA: I know that, but we don't know who she is.

ROCCO: So?

LISA: Never mind, you wouldn't understand.

(ROCCO is rummaging through the big box. He pulls out an envelope.)

ROCCO: Here's something. It's a bunch of names.

LISA: Let me see.

ROCCO: Brian MacDougall, Mary MacDougall, John MacDougall...

LISA: But no Bonnie MacDougall.

(Enter MIKE with BELLE. He enters first as we hear the attic door slam.)

MIKE: Belle, you just slammed the door shut.

BELLE: So?

MIKE: It sticks.

BELLE: How was I supposed to know that?

(MIKE runs to bottom of steps and tries the door. We hear several thuds.)

MIKE: Owwww, my hand!

BELLE: Sorry.

LISA: Hi, Belle.

BELLE: Hi, Lisa. What's Mike doing?

LISA: Getting us in trouble.

MIKE: *(off stage)* Someone come and help me get this door open.

(LISA goes to top of stairs.)

LISA: Mike, shhh, Mom will hear us. Leave it.

(MIKE comes back up.)

MIKE: This is great.

ROCCO: Are there any swords or weapons up here?

(ROCCO starts looking around the attic. LISA has been looking through the envelope.)

MIKE: *(To Rocco)* Be careful, will ya?

LISA: (*Holding envelope*). There's something else in here.

(*LISA empties the contents of the envelope. A letter and some photos fall out.*)

BELLE: Look, pictures!

LISA:(*Looking*) They're old.

BELLE: Look at their clothes. And their hair.

(*ROCCO is still looking around.*)

ROCCO: Any old baseball gloves?

MIKE: No.

(*ROCCO steps on something which cracks.*)

ROCCO: Ooops.

MIKE: Rocco!

(*ROCCO holds up the object he has stepped on.*)

ROCCO: It's okay, it's only a ... I mean *was* only a plastic —

LISA: (*Grabs it*) Squiggles! You squashed Squiggles! I had this when I was little.

ROCCO: Sorry, Squiggles.

(BELLE and LISA are looking through the photos.)

BELLE: Hey, look at this.

(They ALL struggle to read the letter.)

MIKE: (*Reading*) "Let it be known that Bonnie MacDougall, Scottish princess of the highest rite, shall be arriving by boat this said month with the purpose of bringing to her family, the Warners, their due money and family jewels."

BELLE: A Scottish princess! Does that mean you're like, a princess, too?

LISA: I don't know. Maybe. I think so. Yes, I'm probably a princess. I've always felt like a princess.

ROCCO: That would make you a prince, Mike.

BELLE: And this would make your whole family rich. It says "money and family jewels". Oh, Lisa, will you share?

LISA: But why wouldn't Mom tell us about this?

BELLE: Maybe she didn't want you to get too excited.

MIKE: That's probably why she doesn't let us up here.

LISA: No, it's because you're dangerous around glass, Michael, and so you've ruined it for both of us.

ROCCO: Maybe she thought you'd open the presents.

MIKE: Open the presents, an excellent idea!

LISA: Are you crazy?!

MIKE: We could open them, then tape them back. No one would know.

LISA: No way. We'll see them when Bonnie MacDougall gets here.

MIKE: t's already been two years. She may never come. These presents are going to waste.

ROCCO: Mike's right, Lisa. They could rot.

LISA: You read the note: "for as long as it takes."

BELLE: Bonnie MacDougall may never show up. Someone should open them.

ROCCO: Let me. I'm good at this.

(ROCCO takes a gift and shakes it.)

LISA: Careful!

MIKE: You have to open the tape slow so it doesn't rip.

(ROCCO rips the paper wide open on the box.)

ROCCO: Oh, snap.

LISA: Look what you did!

MIKE: Nice going, Rocco.

BELLE: Well, we may as well look inside since Rocco ruined the paper.

MIKE: Lisa, check the door.

LISA: It's stuck shut, remember?

MIKE: Oh, yeah.

BELLE: Maybe your parents will be so worried about you that when they finally do find you up here they won't be mad.

MIKE: Here goes.

(MIKE opens the box and pulls out a smaller box. He opens it.)

BELLE: That's weird, a box in a box in a box.

LISA: What is it, Mike?

MIKE: Another box. Wait, here's a note: "To find the mystery gift, open box number two."

LISA: Mystery?

ROCCO: This is getting good.

LISA: I think we should stop right here.

ROCCO: You gotta do it.

BELLE: Yeah, it's too late to turn back now.

LISA: Then let me open the next one. At least I won't rip the whole thing.

MIKE: Watch what you're doing, Lisa.

BELLE: She knows how to do it.

LISA: (*Unwrapping gift*) You just have to be very careful with the paper, like this.

(LISA opens another gift. She pulls out a small chalkboard and reads from it.)

LISA: "One more gift to go. The last one holds the surprise."

ROCCO: To the jackpot!

BELLE: What do you think is in there?

LISA: No clue.

MIKE: Onward, to the final surprise!

BELLE: I can hardly wait.

(LISA opens the last box. She pulls out an old shoe.)

LISA: A shoe!

ROCCO: An old smelly shoe.

MIKE: What kind of present is that?

BELLE: Look, there's a note with it.

(MIKE pulls it out and reads note.)

MIKE: "Dear Mike and Lisa—"

LISA: Mike and Lisa?

BELLE: That's you guys.

MIKE: *(Still reading)* "Here's the surprise: a shoe. It means shoo, as in get out of the attic where you aren't supposed to be."

LISA: Mom! She trapped us!

ROCCO: Like a mouse. Snap.

LISA: I don't believe it!

MIKE: *(Continues reading)* "I was wondering how long it would take for you two to open these boxes. Now that you've been caught, you can spend Saturday cleaning the garage. Love, Mom. P.S. By the way, Bonnie MacDougall was a real princess. She was my great-great-great-great aunt who lived in a small castle in

Scotland many years ago. But don't wait up, she isn't coming."

LISA: So, we're not royalty?

MIKE: Doesn't look like it.

BELLE: Well, you are, sort of, from a long time ago. I mean, you *are* related to Bonnie MacDougall and she was a princess.

LISA: That's right! We have royal blood! We do!

BELLE: So that makes you guys—

MIKE: Royal servants. Who ever heard of a prince and princess cleaning the garage?

LISA: Good point, your highness!

(THEY all laugh.)

Blackout
The End

SET, PROPS, SOUND and COSTUMES

Happy Birthday, Bonnie MacDougall

SET PIECES

Set can be as simple or as elaborate as you like. The set (attic) holds any attic-type items you can find –trunks, boxes, holiday decorations, etc. but there should be at least two boxes, one marked "Glass/ Fragile" and the other "Dishes".

PROPS

1 cardboard box (to hold wrapped gifts)

3 small wrapped gifts

1 small box inside box #1

Few old photos

Envelope (with names on front and holds photos)

Small, broken plastic toy- any kind (Mr. Squiggles) *

Small chalkboard (or written note if no chalkboard available)

An old shoe of any kind (in box #3)

*Prop Construction Tips

Have the small, cracked toy pre-set before the show under a cloth or newspaper on the floor, along with a pre-set large uncooked pasta shell next to it. The actor portraying Rocco will step on the covered pasta shell to imitate the sound of plastic cracking, but then pull out the pre-set, cracked plastic toy.

COSTUMES
Daily wear

SOUND
Door slamming
Loud thud

DOTTIE'S PARADISE

CAST OF CHARACTERS

REMI BURGER—around 13 years old and oldest Burger sibling.

ALICE BURGER— 9-11 years old.

JERRY BURGER—10-11 years old.

DOTTIE—a rabbit, played by an actor of any age.

PLACE
A city in the U.S.A.

TIME
The present.

SETTING
The family room of the Burger home.

Scene One – A Saturday afternoon in March.

Scene Two – One week later.

Scene Three – Several days later.

DOTTIE'S PARADISE

A family room in the Burger home.

AT RISE: ALICE BURGER has a laptop in front of her. She wears a headset and is watching something funny, laughing aloud every several seconds.

Her brother, JERRY BURGER, is watching TV.

JERRY: Quit it, will ya?

ALICE: Ha, ha, ha!

JERRY: Yo! Alice!

ALICE (*Doesn't hear him*) Ha, ha, ha!!!

JERRY: QUIET!

> (*ALICE pulls off headset.*)

ALICE: What?

JERRY: I can't hear. You're laughing too loud.

ALICE: This is SO funny! You should watch it with me.

JERRY: No thanks.

ALICE: Then go someplace else.

JERRY: News flash, this is the only TV in the house in case you forgot, sister dear, so no, I can't move. But *you* could go anywhere with the laptop.

ALICE: I like it in here.

JERRY: Then watch something not funny.

ALICE: You want to know what's not funny? You, Jerry Burger. I was here longgggg before you came in and turned on the TV.

JERRY: I came in here, like, two minutes after you.

ALICE: I was still here first.

JERRY: Alice, come on!

ALICE: Okay, I'll try to laugh quieter. But it won't be easy – this is very funny.

JERRY: Just try, hyena.

(Enter REMI, carrying pet rabbit supplies. He plops the stuff down.)

JERRY: What's all the rabbit stuff doing here?

REMI: It's Dottie's.

ALICE: I know that, but why is it here?

JERRY: Is she sick?

REMI: No. I'll be right back – I have to go get her.

ALICE: Then what are you doing with her? You never take her out of your bedroom.

REMI: She's off to a new life.

JERRY: What do you mean?

REMI: I mean, ol' Dottie and I are finished. I made a bet with some of the team at basketball that we couldn't beat East Central. I said there was no way, and if we did I'd give one of them my rabbit. Who knew? Scotsville JVs have never beaten East Central. Ever. Till now.

JERRY: That was a good game.

ALICE: Yeah.

REMI: Anyway, Angel Lopez is taking Dottie.

ALICE: You're really giving away your pet rabbit because of a stupid bet?

JERRY: People bet *money*, Remi, not their pets.

REMI: Actually, I don't want Dottie anyway. She doesn't do anything except eat and sleep. Boring, boring, boring.

ALICE: Then why do you even have her?

REMI: You know why! Grandma Burger gave her to me for Christmas. I never asked for a rabbit. I asked for a skateboard and I got a rabbit. How are those two things even slightly similar?

ALICE: That's so mean to just to throw Dottie away like that.

REMI: It's called *relocation*, Alice. A new home. I'm not killing and cooking her for dinner.

JERRY: Are you sure Angel wants Dottie?

REMI: I don't know. I don't care. I'm just glad to finally get rid of her. It's a big load off. So long, Dottie.

ALICE: Poor Dottie!

REMI: Like you care. You never even look at her.

ALICE: Because you won't let us in your room, dummy! "Keep out, get out, get lost". That's all you ever say.

REMI: Well...

JERRY: It's true, Remi.

REMI: You two wouldn't want her either. She does nothing except sit there. I don't know why rabbits even exist.

ALICE: I would take really good care of her. And so would Jerry, right Jer?

JERRY: Yeah.

REMI: Well, too bad, she's going. Angel will be here any minute.

ALICE: You should've made yourself the prize instead of Dottie.

REMI: Ha, ha, ha.

> *(REMI'S cell phone sounds a text.*
> *He reads it and sighs.)*

JERRY: Who's that from?

REMI: Angel can't take Dottie; their mother is allergic.

ALICE: Yay!

REMI: No, not yay! Dottie's going. I've decided. I'm taking her to the animal shelter then.

JERRY: The one on South Street? It's way overcrowded. And they probably don't even take rabbits, just dogs and cats.

REMI: Well they're gonna get a rabbit today.

ALICE: Jerry and I will take her then.

JERRY: (*To Alice*) We will?

ALICE: Yeah. We want her.

JERRY: We do?

ALICE: Jerry and I are always saying: I wish we could own Dottie.

JERRY: We say that?

ALICE: She can stay here in this room since, unlike Remi's gigantic humungous bedroom, both of ours are way too small for a rabbit cage. Mom won't care.

REMI: Go ahead then, but you guys are gonna be sorry. And don't ask me for any rabbit advice. None. You guys are on your own. My rabbit days are over starting right now.

ALICE: (*Sarcastically*) Gee, you have such a big heart.

REMI: I know. Okay, I'll go get her.

(Remi exits.)

JERRY: Nice one, Alice.

ALICE: What?

JERRY: I never said I wished we could own Dottie. In fact, *you* never said it either.

ALICE: I couldn't just let him take Dottie to the shelter. You even said the place is overcrowded.

JERRY: It is.

ALICE: So. we have to do this, Jerry.

JERRY: Well, you'd better look up taking care of a rabbit. Fast.

ALICE: What's to know? All they do is sit and eat and sleep.

JERRY: You better hope that's all.

Blackout
End of Scene One

Scene Two

One week later. JERRY and
ALICE are doing their
homework. In a cage huddles
DOTTIE, a rabbit (actor). The
cage is too small for Dottie.

DOTTIE looks out sadly through
the bars, then begins chewing on
them.

JERRY: She keeps chewing on the bars, look.

ALICE: Maybe they taste good.

JERRY: Did you look up why she's doing that?
You're the one who said we'd take her.

ALICE: You said you'd take her, too.

JERRY: Only because you told Remi I would.

ALICE: At least she gets to stay in the same
house.

JERRY: She's chewed that one bar down to almost nothing. (Beat) Hand me the chips, will you?

> (*ALICE hands JERRY potato chips.*
> *DOTTIE watches him.*)

ALICE: It's your turn to change the straw.

JERRY: No, it isn't. It's your turn.

ALICE: It is not.

JERRY: I did it last time.

ALICE: Nuh-uh.

> (*JERRY picks up a piece of paper and reads.*)

JERRY: Let's see. Tuesday March 20th: Alice changes the straw. I made a chart in case you tried to get out of it.

ALICE: Fine!

> (*JERRY continues eating and*
> *DOTTIE continues staring.*)

ALICE: It looks like she wants a chip. Let's see if she wants one.

JERRY: No! We can't just give her a chip. What if rabbits aren't supposed to eat them? I think they just eat rabbit food.

(Enter REMI.)

ALICE: Hey, Remi.

REMI: So, how are the new rabbit owners, guardians of the Cottontail?

JERRY: Fine. I guess.

REMI: Was I right or what? It's been almost a week now and you can see for yourself how much fun Dottie is, sitting there in her little Paradise, sleeping, eating, eating, sleeping, eating, sleeping.

ALICE: She's more fun than you are.

REMI: Sticks and stones, little sister.

ALICE: Remi, we have a question.

REMI: No rabbit talk.

ALICE: Does Dottie eat potato chips?

JERRY: We need to know.

REMI: All I gave her were those smelly pellets.

ALICE: No lettuce or anything?

REMI: I don't know. Maybe lettuce. Sometimes. I don't know.

JERRY: Well did you or didn't you?

REMI: Look, you guys are on your own. You wanted her, you got her. I told you, my Dottie days are done. Fini.

ALICE: Thanks a lot, Remi.

JERRY: I thought you had practice today.

REMI: I do. I'm going now.

JERRY: It's already 4:30.

ALICE: You're always late for everything.

REMI: What are you, the basketball police? I'm going.

ALICE: Bye.

REMI: Hey, did you guys get the new Play Station yet?

JERRY: No, but we have almost enough money saved up.

REMI: I can't wait.

JERRY: For what? Alice and I saved up for it ourselves. You wouldn't pitch in any money, remember?

ALICE: Yeah, so buy your own Play Station.

REMI: We'll see.

ALICE: Yeah, we will.

REMI: Well, I'm off. Better not keep the team waiting. Let me know when you get the Play Station.

ALICE: Yeah, right.

REMI: Hey, I gave you the rabbit.

ALICE: Bye, Remi.

(REMI exits. ALICE crosses to the cage.)

JERRY: Don't give her any of those chips!

ALICE: I'm not. I'm just gonna change the straw.

(ALICE starts to open the door.
DOTTIE, startled, thumps and moves away.)

JERRY: You're scaring her.

ALICE: No, I'm not. She always does that. Have you ever petted her?

JERRY: No, have you?

ALICE: No. I don't think she likes being petted. She's not very friendly.

(JERRY goes to the cage. THEY both look in.
DOTTIE slowly moves closer to them. DOTTIE
bonks her nose by ALICE'S hand.)

JERRY: What's she doing?

ALICE: I don't know.

JERRY: At least she stopped thumping.

ALICE: I just thought of something Remi said.

JERRY: What's that?

ALICE: That Dottie was in Paradise. (*Pause*) Does this look like Paradise to you?

JERRY: No.

(JERRY goes to the computer and starts typing.)

ALICE: Look, Jer, she's bonking her nose again. What is that?

JERRY: I don't know, but I think it's time we found out.

Blackout
End of Scene Two

Scene Three

Several days later. There's a spacious, long cage along one wall with toys and twigs and decorations hanging from it. There's a sign on the cage that reads: PARADISE.

The cage door is open and DOTTIE is out and hopping around.

JERRY and ALICE are sitting on the floor with her. Dottie hops up to them and they pet her.

ALICE: *(To Dottie)* Hey, girl.

JERRY: Hey, where ya going, huh?

ALICE: Come here, Dottie. Come on.

JERRY: I've got her salad ready.

(DOTTIE, excited, goes to the salad.

They feed it to her.)

ALICE: Did you see how fast she was running around here before? She looked like a dog running in circles.

JERRY: She was doing that this morning, too.

(Enter REMI. Sees cage.)

REMI: What the heck is that?

JERRY: What's it look like?

REMI: A big, expensive cage for a boring rabbit.

JERRY: Well, you got the expensive part right.

ALICE: But the only boring one here is you.

REMI: Ha, ha. Did Mom and Dad buy you that?

JERRY: No, we used our Play Station money to get it.

REMI: You're kidding me?! You used your Play Station money for that?

ALICE: Dottie could hardly move in the cage you had.

REMI: She doesn't do anything, what's the difference?

ALICE: She didn't do anything because she couldn't move.

REMI: What's she doing outside the cage? Did she escape?

JERRY: No, she's running around, playing.

REMI: Playing?

ALICE: Having fun. And eating greens. She wasn't getting the right food before.

JERRY: Or any exercise.

(DOTTIE runs up to JERRY. He pets her and she nuzzles for more pets.)

REMI: You can pet her like a dog or cat?

JERRY: Yeah.

REMI: I never knew that.

JERRY: She likes it.

REMI: How'd you get her to do that? To come by you?

ALICE: We just let her out and waited. It took a couple of days before she trusted us.

JERRY: She was shy at first, but not anymore. Now she likes it.

REMI: I didn't know they like to run around.

ALICE: Do you want to try petting her?

REMI: No.

JERRY: Why not?

REMI: She doesn't like me.

ALICE: Maybe because you never liked her.

(JERRY coaxes DOTTIE to him and REMI. Slowly REMI gets closer to DOTTIE.)

REMI: I don't know.

JERRY: Just try.

REMI: She's probably scared of me.

ALICE: Go on, Remi.

(REMI pets DOTTIE.)

REMI: Hey, she likes it.

ALICE: She does! Look at her.

REMI: How about that?

ALICE: Do you feel how soft her fur is?

REMI: Yeah.

JERRY: Hey, aren't you supposed to be at practice?

REMI: Uh, I'm not going.

JERRY: Why?

REMI: 'Cause.

JERRY: 'Cause why?

REMI: 'Cause - I – a – got cut from playing this week.

ALICE: You did?

REMI: I came late too many times, Coach said.

JERRY: That's too bad.

REMI: He said if I am on time for every practice starting next week, I can come back.

JERRY: You can do that. Be on time.

REMI: Yeah. I know. I will.

ALICE: Do you want to give Dottie some salad?

REMI: Salad?

ALICE: It's her favorite. We looked up what foods to feed her.

REMI: So, Dottie has fresh vegetables—

ALICE: A new cage—

JERRY: And a new water bottle.

REMI: A whole new start.

ALICE: She has something else, too.

REMI: What's that?

ALICE: A new friend.

REMI: Who?

LIGHTS UP!

ALICE: You!

REMI: Naw.

ALICE: Yes.

REMI: You think so?

(DOTTIE rubs up against REMI. THEY all laugh.)

ALICE: Oh, yeah, I think so!

(DOTTIE nuzzles them as light fade.)

Blackout

The End

SET, PROPS, SOUND AND COSTUMES

Dottie's Paradise

Family furniture: chairs, sofa, table, desk, laptop, computer or tablet *

TV *

Small cage *

Large cage * (roomy enough for the "rabbit" actor to move comfortably)

*Set Construction Tips

Sofa: Two or three folding chairs covered with a throw.

Cages: Any loose fencing, screen or netting around an open box; or cut slots in the cardboard box to serve as the bars.

TV and *Computers:* cardboard box construction. The screen will face upstage and unseen by the audience.

PROPS

Headphones or ear buds

Chore chart

Cell phone

Bag of potato chips or other

Rabbit supplies: bowl, bag of "food", straw (optional)*

Bowl of salad greens*

*Prop Construction Tips

Straw: Shredded newspaper

Salad greens: Shredded green paper; green Playdoh or clay; kids' fake food

COSTUMES

Daily wear

Rabbit costume, if available, or just rabbit ears

SOUND EFFECTS

Text sound

THE HEARTS OF PHILLY

CAST OF CHARACTERS

All characters except Sasha are 10-12 years old.

TAYLOR

FRANKIE

PEARL

JILL

LISA

SASHA – 6 or 7 years old.

PLACE

Urban Philadelphia.

TIME

The present. Winter.

SETTING

An old, abandoned building, condemned and marked for demolition.

THE HEARTS OF PHILLY

Inside an old, abandoned
building. A few empty boxes are
beneath some broken and taped
up windows. A sign on the wall
reads: *The Hearts of Philly
Friendship Club.*

Any visible doors are boarded up
and actors enter and exit through
a window Stage Right.

AT RISE: PEARL and JILL are
standing.

TAYLOR is peering out the
window.

TAYLOR: I still don't see her.

PEARL: She'll be here.

TAYLOR: We're only gonna wait five more minutes.

JILL: And then what?

TAYLOR: We start without her.

JILL: We can't start without Frankie.

PEARL: Yeah, it has to be all of us.

TAYLOR: Well, she should be on time.

JILL: Who made you the boss, Taylor? Uh, no one.

PEARL: Yeah, this is a democracy. We wait for her.

TAYLOR: Okay, fine.

(A noise is coming from window.)

FRANKIE: *(off stage)* Go on, Sash, I'm right behind you.

SASHA: *(off stage)* I can't get in.

FRANKIE: *(off stage)* Just push through, Sasha.

JILL: Frankie's here.

PEARL: Somebody's with her.

(Enter FRANKIE and her sister, SASHA, through the window. SASHA has a stuffed penguin.)

TAYLOR: *(To Frankie)* You brought your little sister with you?!!

PEARL: Sure looks like it.

FRANKIE: Hi, guys.

TAYLOR: Hurry up, make sure nobody sees you.

FRANKIE: Move Sasha, so I can get in.

TAYLOR: I can't believe you brought Sasha!

JILL: Yeah, Frankie.

FRANKIE: I had to. My mom got called into work.

PEARL: What are we supposed to do now?

FRANKIE: Same as we always do.

TAYLOR: But now Sasha knows about our secret club.

JILL: And our secret meeting place.

FRANKIE: Sasha won't tell anybody. Right, Sash?

SASHA: Uh-huh.

FRANKIE: *(To others)* It's okay.

TAYLOR: No, it isn't! You know the rules. We agreed, Frankie.

FRANKIE: It's not my fault. My mom got a new job.

(SASHA is sniffling with a cold, sneezes.)

TAYLOR: Watch where you sneeze, will ya?

FRANKIE: It was bring Sasha or not come at all.

TAYLOR: *(Snotty)* Well, thank you, Frankie, thank you for coming— late and bringing your little sister.

SASHA: I'm soooo cold. (*Snee*zes) Ahhhhhh-choooo.

FRANKIE: Quiet, Sasha.

PEARL: Let's just start, okay?

TAYLOR: *(To Sasha)* Not a word of this to anyone, Sasha, including your little friends.

SASHA: Okay.

FRANKIE: She said okay, Taylor. Leave her alone.

TAYLOR: I'm just sayin'.

JILL: Come on everybody.

(THEY gather together in a circle and recite.)

ALL: One soul, one heart, together, together, never to part. Friends who share, friends who dare, friends who always, always care.

(SASHA sniffles loudly.)

TAYLOR: *(To Sasha)* Wipe your nose or something! Geeez.

SASHA: Sorry.

PEARL: First order of business: we have big problem. A giant one. Huge. Colossal. Mountain size.

JILL: Just tell us!!

(PEARL holds up a flyer.)

PEARL: Here. Read this.

FRANKIE: What's it say?

(THEY all struggle to read it.)

TAYLOR: What?! They're tearing down this building?!

JILL: February twenty-first.

FRANKIE: That's in three weeks.

TAYLOR: Where did you get this flyer, Pearl?

PEARL: It was hanging on the fence outside.

TAYLOR: Oh, this is just great.

JILL: That means we only have...three more meetings.

PEARL: Our special place!

FRANKIE: I guess we could meet at each other's houses.

TAYLOR: Right, so everybody would know about our club.

JILL: She's right, Frankie.

PEARL: It's special because *nobody* knows about it.

TAYLOR: Except now Sasha does.

SASHA: I won't tell anybody. Promise.

(sneezes) Ahhhhhh-choooo!

FRANKIE: She won't.

JILL: It doesn't matter anyway.

TAYLOR: We've shared so much under this dirty old roof.

JILL: A whole year and we've never been discovered.

TAYLOR: There must be some way to stop it from being torn down.

JILL: Our secret place going up in a smoke.

PEARL: It just can't!

(SASHA sneezes loudly.)

SASHA: Ahhhhhhhh-choooo.

TAYLOR: *(To Sasha)* Could you sneeze any louder?

FRANKIE: What will we do?

PEARL: I guess the Hearts of Philly will just end.

JILL: I sure will miss you guys.

PEARL: We'll see each around.

JILL: It won't be the same. It's over.

FRANKIE: So, the Hearts of Philly is just finished?

TAYLOR: We've got to figure out something.

(Suddenly there's a rustle from behind some boxes.)

PEARL: What was that?

JILL: It was coming from over there

FRANKIE: Listen.

PEARL: Someone go look.

TAYLOR: Jill, you go.

JILL: I'm not going.

(*SASHA sneezes again.*)

TAYLOR: Stop sneezing! You scared me!

SASHA: Sorry.

TAYLOR: (*Pointing to penguin*) And what is that?

SASHA: Henry, my penguin.

TAYLOR: Who names a penguin Henry?

FRANKIE: (*Defending Sasha*) Sasha does, okay?

TAYLOR: Whatever.

FRANKIE: Just be quiet, Taylor.

PEARL: Hello! Does anybody care that there's a noise coming from over there?!!

JILL: Well, someone go look.

(*There's more noise, then some movement.*)

PEARL: Yeah, somebody.

JILL: Nope.

SASHA: Me either.

FRANKIE: It could be a rat.

PEARL: Or a raccoon.

JILL: Yeah, a rabid raccoon.

TAYLOR: *(Screaming)* Ahhhhhhhhh!!!

(As TAYLOR screams, a figure emerges from behind boxes. Enter LISA.)

FRANKIE: Who are you?

TAYLOR: Yeah, who are you?

PEARL: You totally freaked us out.

JILL: We thought you were a rat.

LISA: I'm Lisa.

TAYLOR: Where did you come from?

LISA: From behind the boxes.

TAYLOR: We know that! But how did you get in here?

LISA: Through the window, like you guys.

JILL: I didn't see you come in.

LISA: I came in before you got here.

TAYLOR: You've been spying on us?

LISA: Not exactly.

TAYLOR: Yes, exactly!

LISA: I was just sitting there.

JILL: Hiding behind the boxes, spying.

PEARL: Very sneaky.

TAYLOR: Well, you're not allowed in here. This is private property.

LISA: No, it isn't. It belongs to the city.

JILL: Did you tell anybody else about this place?

LISA: No.

TAYLOR: Why did you come here?

LISA: I want to join your club.

TAYLOR: What?! No way. We don't even know you.

LISA: I'd really like to join.

TAYLOR: This is a club for *friends*.

LISA: The Hearts of Philly Friendship Club, I know.

TAYLOR: And we're not friends with you.

LISA: You could be.

TAYLOR: Members only.

JILL: It's our secret place.

PEARL: *(To Lisa)* Or *was* our secret place. Now you know about it.

LISA: It's my secret place, too. And I've been watching you. Every Saturday.

TAYLOR: What?!

PEARL: You *are* a spy!

TAYLOR: Incredible.

LISA: Sometimes I just come in here and sit and listen to music.

(SASHA sneezes loudly.)

SASHA: I'm cold, Frankie.

FRANKIE: Zip up your jacket.

LISA: *(To Sasha)* I like your penguin.

SASHA: His name is Henry.

LISA: He looks really special.

SASHA: I got him when I was little. Ahhhhhh-choooo.

LISA: Bless you.

(LISA hands Sasha a tissue.)

SASHA: Thanks.

LISA: *(To others)* So, do you think I could join your club?

TAYLOR: No.

PEARL: *(To Lisa, kindly)* Why don't you start your own friendship club, you know, with your own friends?

LISA: I don't have any friends. Not really. We just moved to Philadelphia.

TAYLOR: Just make some new friends.

LISA: That's what I'm trying to do.

JILL: There isn't going to be a club anymore anyway.

LISA: This doesn't have to be the end.

PEARL: We'll never find a place like this again. It wouldn't be the same anywhere else.

TAYLOR: *(Jumps up)* I think we'd better go. This meeting is weird now.

JILL: We just got here, Taylor.

FRANKIE: We should at least talk about what we're gonna do once this place is gone.

PEARL: It doesn't matter. It looks like our club is going to end.

FRANKIE: You don't know that.

JILL: Yeah, maybe we could find someplace else.

PEARL: This place is just so perfect.

TAYLOR: Let's just leave. I want to go.

LISA: So, can I join your club? I've never been in a club before.

JILL: Um, I don't think so.

LISA: You can vote. I know you guys vote on stuff.

TAYLOR: Something else you learned from spying on us.

PEARL: Maybe we should vote. We do on all the important stuff.

JILL: For three more meetings. What's the point?

TAYLOR: (*To Lisa*) Go over there back by the boxes. And don't listen!

LISA: I won't.

(LISA goes to the far end of the room.)

TAYLOR: Okay, I say no. Even if we weren't losing this place. We don't know her, plus she seems kinda different.

SASHA: I like her.

TAYLOR: You're not voting, Sasha!

JILL: I say no, too.

FRANKIE: You guys are being so unfair.

TAYLOR: We're voting, Frankie.

FRANKIE: We're not *discussing* it. You're just voting.

TAYLOR: Yeah, we are. I vote no.

FRANKIE: She said she doesn't have any friends.

TAYLOR: So.

PEARL: We don't know anything about her.

FRANKIE: We could.

JILL: *(To Frankie)* Why do you want her to join so bad?

FRANKIE: We're a friendship club. What are friends club about then?

TAYLOR: Not inviting strangers to join us.

FRANKIE: You are so mean sometimes, Taylor.

PEARL: Come on you guys. Hearts of Philly is almost dead anyway.

TAYLOR: All in favor of *not* inviting this Lisa in, raise your hand.

(All but FRANKIE raise hands.)

JILL: The no's have it.

PEARL: *(To Lisa)* You can come back now.

(LISA comes back over.)

TAYLOR: Sorry, but we aren't letting in new members, especially since we will be ending soon.

LISA: Okay.

(LISA goes back by the boxes.)

JILL: We just—don't need any more members.

TAYLOR: *(To Lisa)* We voted fair and square and it was no. Sorry.

FRANKIE: Let's get out here. Come on, Sasha. *(Pause)* Bye, Lisa. It was nice meeting you.

SASHA: *(To Lisa)* Good bye.

LISA: Bye.

PEARL: *(To others)* I'm going, too.

FRANKIE: Put on your hat and gloves, Sasha.

SASHA: Okay.

TAYLOR: *(At window)* Move it, move it.

JILL: Okay, geez, Taylor, I'm going.

(LISA stays behind. The others go to the window to exit. SASHA sets Henry down to put on her hat and gloves as others shove out of the window. FRANKIE picks up Henry and shoves him into her coat pocket, but Henry falls out and onto the floor. They exit. After a few moments LISA starts to leave

LIGHTS UP!

*and notices Henry. She goes to window and looks
out.)*

LISA: (*Shouting out window*) Hey, you forgot—

*(Apparently no one is out there, so LISA puts
Henry in her backpack to leave.)*

Blackout

End of Scene One

Scene Two

Fifteen minutes later. FRANKIE
and SASHA rush in through the
window and look around.

SASHA: (*Crying*) Henry! Henry!

FRANKIE: I don't see him.

SASHA: (*Crying*) Henry, where are you,
Henry?!

FRANKIE: We'll look on the sidewalk again.

SASHA: He's gone and it's all your fault!

FRANKIE: I'm sorry, Sasha. We'll find him.

SASHA: No, we won't. He's gone.

Blackout

End of Scene Two

Scene THREE

The following Saturday.
TAYLOR, PEARL AND JILL are
sitting in a circle.

TAYLOR: I can't believe Frankie is late again!

PEARL: Maybe she couldn't come.

JILL: She would've called.

(TAYLOR has crossed to the boxes.)

TAYLOR: At least the spy isn't here.

PEARL: Well, you did tell her she wasn't
wanted.

TAYLOR: So did you! We voted, Pearl. Fair and
square.

PEARL: Okay, okay.

(A noise at the window.)

FRANKIE: (*Yelling*) Help, my coat is stuck on a nail. Somebody help me!

JILL: Finally!

FRANKIE: Just get it off for me.

PEARL: Hold still!

(*FRANKIE and SASHA push in.*)

TAYLOR: (*Referring to Sasha*) What is *she* doing her again?!

FRANKIE: My mom had to work.

TAYLOR: The Hearts of Philly is falling apart right in front of us.

(*SASHA is sad and near tears.*)

JILL: What's wrong, Sasha?

SASHA: I lost Henry, my penguin.

PEARL: Where did you lose him?

FRANKIE: Here. Last week. I had him in my coat pocket and he must have fallen out. We looked a bunch of times on the sidewalk and even back here, but nothing.

TAYLOR: Well, I think it's pretty obvious what happened. That girl Lisa took him. She was the last one in here.

(SASHA starts crying.)

PEARL: You don't know that she took him, Taylor.

TAYLOR: Like totally she did. She was mad that we wouldn't let her join Hearts of Philly, and she saw the teddy bear—

SASHA: Penguin!

TAYLOR: —and picked him and took him.

JILL: We don't know where she lives either.

FRANKIE: And thanks to you guys, she'll never come back after the way you ditched her.

SASHA: *(Crying)* I want Henry!

FRANKIE: *(To others)* She's been crying all week.

TAYLOR: Another Hearts of Philly meeting ruined. Great.

PEARL: Come on, let's just make our circle.

(They gather in a circle.)

ALL: One soul, one heart, together, together, never to part. Friends who share, friends who dare, friends who always, always care.

JILL: Any ideas on a new place?

PEARL: No.

FRANKIE: Me neither. Taylor?

TAYLOR: No.

(Enter LISA through window.)

SASHA: It's that girl!

TAYLOR: I can't believe you came back here.

JILL: Even after we voted against you.

LISA: I'm not here for that. I just wanted to give this to Sasha.

(LISA pulls Henry out of backpack. SASHA grabs it from her, hugging it.)

SASHA: Henry, Henry, Henry!!

TAYLOR: See? I told you she stole it! I told you!

PEARL: Taylor, stop.

LISA: I found it on the floor but you guys were already gone, so I took him home so it didn't get lost.

FRANKIE: Thank you so much. My sister was so sad.

SASHA: *(To Lisa)* You're the best! You're a good friend. You brought Henry back! I missed him so much.

LISA: Henry missed you, too, Sasha.

PEARL: That was really nice to bring him back.

JILL: Yeah, it was. Wasn't it, Taylor.

(TAYLOR is silent.)

FRANKIE: Taylor?

TAYLOR: Yeah.

LISA: I'm gonna go now.

(LISA gets to the window and stops.)

174

LISA: There's a wooden shed behind the old library that nobody uses. You guys could meet there. You should check it out.

(LISA starts through the window.)

FRANKIE: Wait! Come back.

JILL: What are you doing, Frankie?

(LISA steps back in.)

FRANKIE: Even after we voted not to let you join us you told us about a new place.

LISA: Yeah, that's okay. I know you voted — fair and square.

JILL: And you took care of Henry and brought him back here for Sasha.

PEARL: Sasha is right.

FRANKIE: Huh?

PEARL: What Sasha just said before, that Lisa was a good friend. She is. Isn't that what real friends do, help each out?

JILL: Yeah.

PEARL: We're the ones who didn't act like friends should. We wouldn't even give you a chance.

TAYLOR: And so, if you are still interested, we would like if you would join the Hearts of Philly.

LISA: Don't you have to all vote on it first?

TAYLOR: All in favor?

ALL: Yes!!

SASHA: How about me?

ALL: No!

FRANKIE: Sasha never blabbed to anybody about us or this place.

PEARL: That's true.

JILL: (To *Sasha*) Promise to leave Henry home next time?

SASHA: Promise!

TAYLOR: Oh, why not? It's a brand-new Hearts of Philly. All in favor?

ALL: Yes! (*All make a circle*) One soul, one heart, together, together, never to part. Friends who share, friends who dare, friends who always, always care.

Blackout
The End

SET, PROPS
AND COSTUMES

The Hearts of Philly

SET PIECES

Boxes stacked up (Lisa hides behind)

Sign: Poster size with "Hearts of Philly Friendship Club"

Yellow tape with "Construction" or "Danger" or "Construction Area" *

Old table or stool (optional)

*Set Construction Tip

If official yellow tape is not available, masking tape or duct tape will work.

PROPS

Stuffed penguin (or another stuffed animal)

Flyer announcing date of demolition

Tissue

Backpack

COSTUMES

Winter wear: jackets, hats. Sasha has gloves or mittens.

A PENNY FOR YOUR THOUGHTS

CAST OF CHARACTERS

GABI— 7-8 years old or younger, kind and understanding.

ROBIN— 8-9 years old, snotty and bossy.

JAMIE—7-8 years old, has an injured arm, kind.

PLACE

A city in the U.S.A.

TIME

The present.

SETTING

A schoolyard.

A PENNY FOR YOUR THOUGHTS

A schoolyard. A large rock sits to the side.

AT RISE: GABI is talking to ROBIN. Robin is wearing a Chicago Cubs cap and flipping a penny in the air and catching it. (Note: the penny should be mimed and left to the audience's imagination to see.)

Sitting alone by the rock is JAMIE, in an arm cast and sling.

GABI: You should have seen this bat, Robin. It just kept flying around in circles right over my bed. I was screaming so loud.

ROBIN: Why?

GABI: Why what?

ROBIN: Why were you screaming?

GABI: Because there was a bat in my bedroom!

ROBIN: So.

GABI: So? it was a *bat*. A yukky flying rat with big wings and it was in my bedroom.

ROBIN: Baby.

GABI: I am not a baby. You would have screamed, too, if you had a bat in your bedroom.

ROBIN: First of all, *I* would have left the bedroom, and second, even if I didn't, I wouldn't have screamed. It makes the bat more scared.

GABI: How do you know?

ROBIN: Because I know a lot about bats. They're gross, dangerous animals and a menace to society.

GABI: A – what?

ROBIN: Bats are dangerous.

GABI: They're ugly, but I don't think they're dangerous.

ROBIN: Yes, they are.

GABI: Since when do you know so much about bats?

ROBIN: Since forever, Gabi. Don't bother trying, you could never keep up with me.

GABI: Could too.

ROBIN: Did you get the bat out?

GABI: Yeah, my mom threw a blanket over it and put it outside.

(ROBIN is flipping the penny as they talk.)

GABI: Hey, Robin, show me how to flip a penny like that.

ROBIN: No, it's too hard; you could never learn.

GABI: I could try. Please.

ROBIN: No, it's a talent. It takes months to learn how to do it and not drop it.

LIGHTS UP!

(ROBIN misses the penny on the throw and watches it roll off Stage Right.)

GABI: There goes your penny.

ROBIN: Thanks a lot, Gabi, it's all your fault!

GABI: I didn't make you do that.

(ROBIN stomps off to get the penny. JAMIE gets up and crosses to GABI.)

JAMIE: Hi.

GABI: Hi.

JAMIE: I'm Jamie.

GABI: I've seen you in school. Mr. Ramone's class.

JAMIE: I heard you guys talking about bats.

GABI: There was one in my bedroom.

JAMIE: I know. I would have been scared, too.

GABI: You would have?

JAMIE: Yeah, but bats aren't bad. They eat insects and pollinate flowers.

GABI: I knew it! I knew they weren't bad!

JAMIE: Creepy looking, though.

GABI: What happened to your arm?

JAMIE: I fell off my bike.

GABI: Does it hurt?

JAMIE: Not much.

GABI: Yeah. Hey, can you flip a penny?

JAMIE: I don't think so.

GABI: Me either. Robin can.

JAMIE: We could learn.

GABI: Robin won't show me.

JAMIE: So. We can do it ourselves.

GABI: Can you, with that thing on?

JAMIE: I'll use my other hand.

(Enter ROBIN with the penny,
then stares at JAMIE.)

ROBIN: Who's that?

LIGHTS UP!

GABI: This is Jamie.

(*JAMIE moves toward ROBIN.*)

JAMIE: (*Referring to cap*) Hey, Chicago Cubs! That's my favorite team.

ROBIN: My father bought it for me.

JAMIE: Cool.

ROBIN: He's taking me to a Cubs game.

JAMIE: That's awesome! You're so lucky.

GABI: Hey, Robin, Jamie can't flip a penny, either.

ROBIN: (*Referring to Jamie's arm*) No kidding. He's got a cast on and it's in a–

JAMIE: Sling. But that's not why I can't flip a penny. I just don't know how. Yet.

ROBIN: Well *I'm* not showing you. Gabi couldn't learn either.

GABI: You would never show me how!

ROBIN: Whatever.

(ROBIN exits, flipping the penny.)

GABI: (*Yells*) Thanks a lot, Robin.

JAMIE: You know, you can learn anything you want to — flip a penny, ride a bike. Anything!

GABI: Can you ride your bike, with the cast on?

JAMIE: Not for two weeks. Hey, I'll bet you can balance on one foot, on that rock.

GABI: I've never done that.

JAMIE: Me either.

GABI: I don't want to try.

JAMIE: Come on.

GABI: Won't we fall?

JAMIE: I don't know.

*(JAMIE hops up on the rock
and balances on one foot.)*

GABI: You're so high up.

JAMIE: Just put your hands out like this. For balance. I can put one arm out.

GABI: You're doing it!

JAMIE: Come on up.

GABI: That's all right.

JAMIE: I did it. Come on! Try it.

GABI: Oh, okay.

(GABI gets up on the rock.)

JAMIE: Stand with both feet flat at first. When you feel steady, lift one foot way up, like this.

GABI: This is fun. I'm an airplane! Yay!

(ROBIN sneaks up to scare GABI.)

ROBIN: Booooo!

(Startled, GABI yells and falls. JAMIE, startled, falls backwards, but recovers.)

GABI: Ahhhhhh! Help! Owwww.

(ROBIN rushes to GABI.)

ROBIN: Gabi, I – I – I was just kidding.

JAMIE: (To Gabi) Are you okay?

GABI: *(Upset, to Jamie)* I'm fine. But see, I can't do ANYTHING!!

(GABI runs off.)

JAMIE: Gabi, wait!

Blackout

End of Scene One

Scene Two

The next day. GABI sits alone
against the rock, flipping a penny
and catching it. Enter JAMIE.

JAMIE: Hi.

GABI: Hi. Hey, I can flip a penny.

JAMIE: You can?

GABI: Yeah, watch.

JAMIE: That's really good.

GABI: You have to keep practicing. Like this.
Here, you try.

(GABI hands JAMIE a penny.)

JAMIE: No, that's okay.

GABI: Why not?

JAMIE: Cause.

GABI: 'Cause why?

JAMIE: 'Cause I don't know how to do it.

GABI: You can do anything you want to. That's what you said yesterday.

JAMIE: I guess so.

GABI: So, try flipping the penny.

JAMIE: How did you get Robin to show you?

GABI: I didn't. I taught myself.

JAMIE: That's cool.

GABI: Try it.

(*JAMIE flips it in the air and drops it.*)

JAMIE: I dropped it.

(*GABI hands JAMIE another penny.*)

GABI: Try again. Pitch it way up in the air.

JAMIE: Like this?

GABI: Snap your wrist when you throw it.

LIGHTS UP!

(JAMIE repeats the actions, dropping again, but then catches it.)

JAMIE: I got it!

GABI: I know, let's flip pennies balancing on one foot.

JAMIE: Okay.

(THEY get up on the rock.)

GABI: It doesn't seem as high up here as yesterday.

(Enter Robin.)

ROBIN: What are you guys doing?

JAMIE: Balancing on one foot.

GABI: And flipping pennies. You know, that thing that takes "months of practice" to learn?

ROBIN: I knew you could learn it right away.

GABI: So why did you keep saying I wouldn't be able to?

ROBIN: I wanted something special that nobody else could do.

JAMIE: I don't have a Cubs cap and you do. Your cap's special because your dad got it for you.

(ROBIN takes off cap.)

ROBIN: No, he didn't.

GABI: You said he did.

ROBIN: I found it on the ground.

(ROBIN hands the cap to JAMIE.)

ROBIN: Here, take it. It's your favorite team.

JAMIE: Really? Thanks!

GABI: Do you guys want to have a contest? See who can flip a penny the highest? I have a bunch of pennies in my pocket.

ROBIN: No.

JAMIE: Why?

GABI: Are you afraid we might throw higher than you?

ROBIN: No, first I want you guys to show me how to balance on the rock with one foot.

GABI: And if you start to fall, we'll catch you.

ROBIN: Promise?

(GABI and JAMIE look at each other and smile.)

GABI and JAMIE: Promise!

Blackout
The End

SET, PROPS
and COSTUMES

A Penny for Your Thoughts

SET PIECES

Large Rock or Mound *

*Set Construction Tips

Rock: Styrofoam, layers of foam core or polystyrene construction. You can find many examples online. Paper Mache can be applied over the "rock", then painted. Be sure the surface is flat and stable enough to hold the actors safely. If that isn't possible, a large, sturdy box will do. For extra safety, a step stool can be placed behind the "rock" to get up more easily. Safety first! And if none of the above is possible, actors can mime the height. If they believe they're high up, the audience will, too.

PROPS

Arm cast *

Arm sling *

Penny is mimed

*Prop Construction Tips

A "plaster" arm cast can be made from layers of toilet paper wrapped around the arm, then misted lightly with water to pat it down. Once dry, apply sticky gauze bandage around the paper. Cut the cast enough for the actor to get in and out of, and secure with more sticky gauze before each performance.

An arm sling can be made from a cut piece of cloth in the shape of a triangle, large enough to fit under the arm and over the neck of the actor. Scarves will also work.

COSTUMES

Daily wear

Chicago Cubs cap (or team of choice)

ABOUT THE AUTHOR

Margo Haas is a playwright, actor and novelist. She works in her native state of Ohio teaching playwriting and acting workshops in local schools and theatres. Her published plays and books include adult, teen and young adult mysteries and comedies. Her novel, *In This Sleep of Death*, a teen mystery, is currently being adapted for stage. She lives in Westlake, Ohio with her husband and three very spoiled stray cats.

Contact Margo:
Web: margohaas.com
Email: haasmargo@gmail.com

Made in the USA
Coppell, TX
02 August 2022

80816782R00108